Saying 'THANKS'

Implementing Effective Workplace Recognition

Sue Glasscock
Kimberly Gram

Becoming the Best Report Series

IFS International Ltd.

1995

Sue Glasscock and Kimberly Gram are leading management consultants, specializing in implementing effective employee recognition systems. Their Colorado-based Positive Strokes develops and delivers processes, methods and tools for creating corporate cultures which encourage employee creativity and innovation, enabling individuals to operate at their highest possible performance levels.

Sue and Kimberly speak frequently at international conferences – the Association for Quality and Participation has recognized their 'Saying Thank You' presentation as the "Best of the Best." Their employee recognition system implemented at StorageTek has been acclaimed as Best Practice, and has been benchmarked by over 30 US companies.

Sue Glasscock and Kimberly Gram may be contacted at:

Positive Strokes
5023 West 120th Avenue #128
Broomfield, Colorado 80020
United States

Tel: (303) 420-7311
Fax: (303) 469-9547

British Library Cataloging-in-Publication Data

A catalog record for this book is available from the British Library.

ISBN: 1-85907-022-1

Wolseley Business Park,
Kempston, Bedford MK42 7PW, UK.

Photo-typeset by A. J. Latham Ltd., Houghton Regis, Dunstable, UK.

Printed by Information Press, Oxford, UK.

This book is dedicated
with the deepest love and
the greatest appreciation
to our families

Jim Glasscock

Jack and Peggy Gram

Leon and Helen Shafer

and

Dustin, Jessica, Todd, Beau and Kelly

THANK YOU!

Contents

Introduction

"There is nothing else that so kills the ambitions of a person as criticisms from superiors. I never criticize anyone. I believe in giving a person incentive to work. So, I am anxious to praise, but loath to find fault. If anything, I am hearty in my approbation and lavish in my praise."

Charles Schwab

Why We Need Recognition

The dawning of the high-tech information age has caused today's world to become more and more impersonal. Take a moment to consider the communication methods you experienced during the last week. Many of you probably sent or received communication using the following tools:

- FAX.
- Voice mail.
- Electronic mail.
- Computerized bills.
- Automatic banking transaction.
- Computer network message.
- Satellite transmission.
- Interoffice memo.
- Form letter.
- Teleconference.
- Correspondence with stamped signature.
- Telephone tape recording.

These examples and more illustrate how we have isolated ourselves from human contact and relationships. United Airlines has a television commercial which emphasizes how the airline had lost an old customer by growing too impersonal in its business dealings. As a result of the feedback, the manager is distributing tickets to his employees to personally visit their customers. The last ticket is his, to visit the customer that was lost. The methods mentioned above have made us more efficient communicators. They are cheaper and faster than other options. But, if we solely depend on these methods, what will replace our need for human contact and the benefits we gain from investing in personal relationships?

John Naisbitt addresses this issue in his book *Megatrends*, stating: "We must learn to balance the material wonders of technology with the spiritual demands of our natures." The human spirit is driven by appreciation and feeling good about ourselves, both of which are achieved by positive interaction with others. We are social creatures. So, while these high technology communication tools have become the norm, we still possess our human need to have positive and personal interactions with others.

Consider the things we have done to make our work life easier. We have our personal computers, state of the art copiers, thousands of forms and standard documents . . . every high-tech appliance and piece of paper one could ask for (maybe a few hundred extras!). We have government controls on our safety, employment, environment, health and so forth. There are ergonomically correct chairs, work stations and keyboards. What could possibly be missing from this picture of a wonderful work environment?

Perhaps trust, respect, dignity, self-worth, warmth, sincerity and all of those interpersonal qualities that evolve from investing in long-term mutually beneficial relationships. Are these investments too 'inefficient' for these times? Do we really want our work life to be this impersonal? Are we becoming ineffective communicators by relying too heavily on high-tech tools? Is this just another case of schedule taking precedence over quality?

The majority of current recognition systems rely upon the first-line manager's initiative and knowledge of recognition and motivation. The following example shows what happens when the responsibility for recognition is given to one person. Upon completion of a major project on which one employee expended all of her 'blood, sweat and tears' for no personal credit, she waited patiently for a 'thanks' from the boss. One week went by. Two weeks went by, and still there was no note, compliment or token of emotional support. Finally, in a staff meeting, the boss enthusiastically spoke of the positive feedback received on the project and recognized another individual on the staff for the accomplishment. The employee thought that the manager was a 'good' person with good intentions, but the truth was after working three years in the same department, she did not know! About 99.8% of what the manager thought of the employee's performance was expressed during an annual performance evaluation. It was obvious there was some confusion over who was doing what. Unfortunately, this type of work interaction is not the exception, it is the general rule.

Another well-meaning manager decided to recognize a team of six for a quality improvement project which had yielded significant results in the department. Feeling well-informed on which team members had the most influence and had carried the greatest work load during the project, the decision was made to give three $100 cash awards and three $50 cash awards as a 'thank you' to the team. Needless to say, the $100 recipients were thrilled and the $50 recipients were shocked, disappointed and demotivated. The team had worked together efficiently and effectively with dramatic results. But, this management error in judgment ensured that this team would probably never work together successfully again.

Stephen Covey, in *Seven Habits of Highly Effective People*, talks about a P/PC principle (production/production capability) as it applies to organizational effectiveness. He states:

> *"There are organizations that talk a lot about the customer and then completely neglect the people that deal with the customer – the employees. The PC principle is to always treat your employees exactly as you want them to treat your best customers.*
>
> *You can buy a person's hand, but you can't buy his heart. His heart is where his enthusiasm is, his loyalty. You can buy his back, but you can't buy his brain. That's where his creativity is, his ingenuity, his resourcefulness.*
>
> *PC is treating employees as volunteers just as you treat your customers as volunteers, because that's what they are. They volunteer the best part – their hearts and minds."*

The majority of us spend over one-half of our waking hours at work. Unfortunately, most of us undergo a personality change as soon as we arrive at work. Our job descriptions do not call for common sense, common courtesy, honesty, sincerity, gratitude or being personable, so we abandon these personal attributes in the parking lot. Most corporate strategic goals do not include quality of work life plans to drive improvement in employee satisfaction, morale, the attrition rate or the work environment. Do we think that creativity, loyalty, dependability, trustworthiness and initiative are of a lower priority than stock prices, market share, the reliability of our products, the quality of our services, and the cycle time of our processes? Do we think by establishing these tangible corporate goals, the values and principles required of the work force will naturally follow? Maybe we think competitive compensation packages will ensure these personal attributes or that we can buy the personal qualities required by a successful business operation. But, these 'personal' processes are no different than any other corporate process and result. Effective recognition is critical to creating an environment that breeds creativity and innovation. Recognition, like all other corporate processes, requires constant attention, improvement, monitoring and maintenance (plan, do, check and act). As with any relationship we have outside of work, building effective relationships with suppliers, customers, peers, management, subordinates, benchmarking partners and our professional networks requires constant care to guarantee success. It is a matter of survival. Our competitiveness depends on this ability.

Establishing an effective recognition system is vital to reinforcing the behaviors and activities necessary to ensure the personal principles and practices required to be a viable and successful business operation. The ingredients are not magical or a mystery to any of us. Most of us have applied these recognition techniques in situations outside of the workplace. For example:

- Training the family dog.
- Potty training our children.
- Coaching a child's sports team.

- Thanking a friend or relative for a gift.
- Teaching a class or being a student.
- Participating in Scouts.

All of these personal activities involve the use of positive reinforcement to change or encourage a behavior or skill. In most cases, the positive reinforcement is simply sincere appreciation accompanied with a small token – a dog biscuit, a popsicle, a hug, a trophy, a thank you card, a smiley face sticker or a merit badge. None of these tokens of appreciation are extravagant, for there is truth to the old adage, "It is not the gift, it's the thought that counts." I still have a 'pretty rock' my oldest son gave me for Mother's Day over 10 years ago when he was in kindergarten.

Why do we abandon the practice of sincere appreciation when we come to work? Saying 'thank you' is much more than a social amenity – it is an extremely valuable business tool. Tom Peters dedicated one entire syndicated business column to saying 'thank you'. He states, "The handwritten thank you is a modest act of engagement. It probably won't save lives, but it just might boost your odds of becoming rich, famous and adored. (Not to mention making you feel a lot better about yourself)." He shares the story of a former boss who religiously spent 15 minutes at the end of each day to write about a half-dozen paragraph-long notes to people who had given him time during the day or made a provocative remark in a meeting. Peters shares that this manager became highly successful in his career. The article challenges the reader to try this end-of-the-day ritual for one month, guaranteeing 'amazing' results.

Recognizing work efforts is critical to sustaining motivation and the quality of work life. It helps make work, not only bearable, but enjoyable. The more that recognition is woven into our work days, the more its results can be seen in productivity, profitability and morale. There are many new management and work initiatives to implement in the 1990s, including self-directed work teams, benchmarking, reengineering, ISO 9000 and every other quality or productivity process we choose to adopt. Frankly, implementing any new initiative is a challenge that cannot be met efficiently and effectively without the proper recognition system. In most situations, we have the same 'players' but an entirely different 'ball game'. We know these new approaches are the right way to operate. We know we will reap great benefits. In order to get from 'here to there', and implement the new strategies and methods of operation which will keep our businesses competitive, we need to train in appropriate relationship skills and techniques, and equip ourselves with tools for effective recognition.

Ask any parent, school teacher, coach or psychologist. Positive and immediate reinforcement is the key to changing an existing behavior or teaching a new one. Human beings respond to appreciation, acknowledgment and approval. People *are* a company's most valuable resource. The quality of work life should be our top priority and the personal responsibility of every individual in the workplace. We must stop changing our hats in the workplace, for we still possess all of our basic needs when we are at work. We cannot abandon this need to feel appreciated at the company's front door.

Recognition plays an important role for all of us. It is important that we give and receive recognition for steady consistent efforts, as well as outstanding efforts. Success should be celebrated for meeting expected goals and for accomplishing the unexpected. Recognition is very emotional and personal for both the giver and receiver. For this reason, our intent is to help you establish a framework which allows *all* employees to participate in the recognition process. The following chapters will outline the who, what, when, where and how associated with establishing a positive work climate with recognition being instrumental in driving the behaviors and practices vital to the success of the business.

This book provides processes, methods and tools needed to give the heartfelt, warm and immediate appreciation that encourages the personal attributes individuals need to be creative and innovative, to operate at their highest possible performance level and to have pride in their work contributions.

The Benefits of an Effective Recognition System

The benefits of providing good methods and practices for recognition in the workplace are extensive. They are comparable to the benefits of any positive reinforcement you have seen applied and are an invaluable tool to teach new behaviors or change existing ones. The fast pace and volatility of the marketplace demands we have the ability to change and learn quickly.

As you can see by the following list of benefits, recognition can be the critical instrument to facilitate this learning. Using recognition effectively and appropriately:

- Reinforces desired behaviors, practices, principles and values.
- Gives us a mechanism to show appreciation and say 'thanks'!
- Builds self-esteem and morale.
- Promotes trust and respect.
- Fosters change.
- Drives improvement.
- Celebrates success.
- Improves the quality of work life.
- Motivates individuals and teams to do their best.
- Enhances loyalty.
- Creates a positive attitude and confidence that carries to dealings with customers and suppliers.
- Addresses the basic human need to feel appreciated.
- Reflects commitment to others in our organization.
- Inspires accomplishment and achievement.

- Empowers individuals and teams.
- Encourages teamwork.
- Builds faith.
- Drives out fear.
- Impacts the bottom-line positively.

Chapter 1

Recognition Defined

"The deepest principle in human nature is the craving to be appreciated."

William James

"I have yet to find the person, however great or exalted his station, who did not do better work and put forth greater effort under a spirit of approval *than he would ever do under a spirit of criticism."*

Charles Schwab

"To give real service you must add something which cannot be bought or measured with money, and that is sincerity and integrity."

Donald A. Adams

What Recognition *Really* Means

The Random House College Dictionary defines recognition as:

1. The act of recognizing someone or something.
2. The state of being recognized.
3. The perception or *acknowledgment* of something as true or valid.
4. *Appreciation* of achievements, merit, services, etc., or an expression of this.
5. Formal acknowledgment conveying *approval*.

Recognition in the workplace should always include all three As – *acknowledgment, appreciation and approval*. We have defined the purpose or mission of recognition as follows:

> *"To acknowledge and appreciate those behaviors and practices that establish a working environment that promotes the concepts of loyalty, belonging, confidence, self-worth, teamwork, respect, creativity and trust through frequent and sincere methods of approval."*

There are several methods and tools available for recognition. Regardless of the method selected, the recognition should incorporate seven basic characteristics. The recognition must be sincere, fair and consistent, timely, frequent, flexible, appropriate and specific. The following shows how each characteristic impacts the recognition:

1. Recognition must be *sincere*.

   Have you ever noticed that when corporate budgets are cut, the first programs to be reduced are training and recognition? And yet, at those hundreds of meetings, in corporate documentation and in management presentations, we have been told over and over, "Our employees are our most valuable resource." Well, guess what? The employees are not buying it! They would rather see a sermon than hear one. Great leaders honestly feel and know that their business could not survive without the work and commitment of their people. This knowledge should be reflected in every policy, practice, principle and action the leaders demonstrate. When times are hard, do we abandon our principles, values and beliefs? Do we think that our innate need to be appreciated disappears? *No!* We need it even more. We need to reinforce even small wins to ensure the tide turns. Maybe the tools change, for example, a formal dinner becomes an on-site barbecue with management cooking. The importance of recognition is not in the 'gift', it is the 'thought' that counts. The heartfelt, warm and *sincere* appreciation is what drives creativity, productivity and the willingness to operate at the highest performance levels.

2. The recognition must be *fair and consistent*.

The story goes, "The squeaky wheel gets the grease." Recognition loses its power and value if it is perceived as inequitable and inconsistently applied. In *People, Performance, and Pay*, Carla O'Dell reveals that the majority of current recognition processes and programs in the United States are management-driven with less than five percent of corporate populations receiving recognition. This makes perfect sense, since managers only have two legs, two eyes and two ears, and often facilitate operations between buildings, regions and even countries. Naturally, the employee who brags the loudest or longest, or has a high impact financially, gets noticed. Kin Hubbard once said: "There's no secret about success. Have you ever known a successful man who didn't tell you about it?" Everyone in the workplace makes a contribution and each individual should have an equal opportunity to receive recognition. The intent of the processes in this book is to make recognition everyone's responsibility, to show how to establish a recognition system which creates an environment where all behaviors and practices contributing to the vision and goals of the business operation are positively reinforced, as well as to define the appropriate levels suitable to specific situations.

3. Recognition must be *timely*.

   The more immediate the recognition, the more likely the behavior will be repeated. This concept is vital to using any type of positive reinforcement. What do you think your house would look like if you waited until the end of the year to praise your new dog and give him a dog biscuit for barking to get outside during those 'critical moments'? If you want to give a celebration, an award or a token of appreciation later, that's fine. Just remember to give the praise and thanks immediately.

   Immediate recognition is critical for the following reasons:

   - The noteworthy act is still clear in the minds of the giver and receiver.
   - You don't accidentally forget to recognize by waiting for an occasion.
   - The recognition is more meaningful.
   - Recognition is more likely to be remembered and the behavior or practice is more likely to be repeated.
   - There is more emotion and feeling the closer the recognition is to the occurrence.

4. Recognition must be *frequent*.

   So often, corporate recognition programs are created with only 'administrative ease' in mind. Providing everyone with a Thanksgiving or Christmas turkey is a nice gesture, but it is *not* recognition. It takes a minimum of planning and execution (4000 employees = 4000 turkeys/order in October). A nice form letter complete with the CEO's stamped signature usually accompanies the gift, thanking the employee for the past year of service. What is wrong with this picture? What are some of the messages this form of so-called recognition sends?

   > "Yippee! If I can stick it out in this thankless job another year, I can get another turkey!"
   >
   > "Gee, my co-worker was undependable and did low quality work and he/she gets the same thanks I do!"
   >
   > "If it wasn't a holiday, they probably wouldn't thank me at all!"
   >
   > "Thanks for a year of service? You don't even know my name!"

   This method does not feel like sincere appreciation. It does not reinforce or recognize any *specific* behavior or practice unless it is meant to recognize just being in the workplace at some time, doing something, somewhere, somehow in the last year.

   Saying thanks and showing appreciation should be a daily activity at a minimum. Saying 'thank you' is not a great investment and should be applied liberally! The benefits from frequent, sincere appreciation can positively impact every bottom-line measurement – productivity, sales, product and service quality, customer satisfaction, employee turnover, and so forth.

Recognition should be a habit, part of every employee's training. Every manager should become a role model, exemplifying the principles required to establish mutually satisfying and beneficial work relationships.

Service awards are another example of an 'easy way out'. Ten good years, one employee works and slaves at a company and they are granted the privilege of selecting an award out of a catalog which arrives in the mail with the infamous form letter. The award has a perceived value of $100. The corporation probably pays $75. Lets figure that out! $7.50 for each year of dedication. Fifteen cents a week is the investment. *Wow! How special!* Any system that is this automatic, detached and impersonal should not be considered 'recognition'.

An outstanding approach was started by a vice president of a research and development organization who wanted to get in touch with all of the people in his organization. He calls it the 'Lunch with Dave' program. Two or three times per week (this is a major time commitment for a VP), he selects two or three individuals in his organization to take to lunch. This may sound pretty casual, but Dave researches to find out what these individuals contribute in their everyday work. During the lunch, Dave relates how their work positively impacts the organization's vision, mission, goals and objectives. He also shares his personal vision for the group, what his contributions are and what's happening in other corners of the corporation. Dave carefully remembers the suggestions made and input received, following up with a handwritten note, E-mail or phone call. This is *tons* more work than sending everyone a Christmas card. It happens frequently. What benefits does 'Lunch with Dave' have that the turkey and the service award will never realize?

- *Employee loyalty.*

  Dave is sincere and it shows. Good employees are very valuable, the most important corporate resource. But, employees are mobile volunteers. It is critical that there is an appreciative environment to slow attrition. The company's biggest revenue producing idea could walk out the door for a better offer.

- *Dave knows his organization inside-out.*

  And all of Dave's organization knows him. He doesn't hide in an ivory tower.

- *Dave makes each and every contributor feel important.*

  Whether you are a secretary or a development engineer, you know how you contribute to the big picture.

- *Dave 'walks the talk'.*

  Recognition obviously is a priority in his work schedule.

5. Recognition must be *flexible*.

Corporate recognition programs often involve only one or two tools. By providing a variety of methods for showing appreciation, you ensure the needs of both the giver and recipient can be met. That is what is important. For instance, one company offered a gift certificate for a $100 dinner for two at a very fancy dining establishment. When a manufacturing associate received this award, he shared that he struggled just to put food on the table for his family and could never spend $100 on one dinner with a clear conscience. Even though the majority of recipients loved this certificate, it was redesigned to include a merchandise and gift certificate option. Recognition is a personal and emotional matter, making it critical to ensure enough flexibility to meet the recipient's needs.

6. The recognition must be *appropriate.*

   The recognition method selected should match the effort expended, the behavior exemplified or the results achieved. One company's practice was to bring together everyone who had a suggestion or an idea implemented in one year at a large banquet. Every person was given a coffee mug and a stadium blanket, and toward the end of the dinner grand prizes were awarded in a random drawing. You can almost guess what happened. The employee who suggested a minor area improvement with no actual savings won a trip. The employee who had an idea for a productivity improvement which realized an annual saving of $300,000 went home with the mug, the stadium blanket and a bad attitude. It is critical to provide a thoughtful structure that ensures the right recognition goes to the right situation. It should *never* be a lottery!

7. The recognition must be *specific.*

   Recipients should know exactly what they are being thanked for and why this contribution is valuable. After one team facilitator spent months setting up an interview with another company on customer satisfaction information systems including developing the survey, arranging a room and teleconferencing, establishing the contact with the other company, etc., one of the members of the interviewing team left a voice mail saying, "Thank you! You made my day!" The facilitator was delighted, but could not figure out how this compliment had been accomplished. Was it the refreshments? Later, the facilitator called the team member back and asked. He related that the questions had led to answers which reaffirmed his personal values and principles important to operating in a customer service environment. If the questions had not included the human factors and actual customer philosophy, as well as the hardware and software used, an important message would have been missed. After realizing specifically what had been done and how accidentally it had happened, the facilitator decided to standardize this approach when conducting research. Now, the philosophy, practices and processes that drive the technology are always included.

Acknowledgment, appreciation and approval are all required to qualify an action as 'recognition'. A form letter is an acknowledgment, but lacks sincere appreciation or a demonstration of approval for a specific behavior or practice. Christmas turkeys or service awards acknowledge an employee's presence, but not much more. The missing ingredient in these recipes is what makes individuals want to change, want to be their best and want to come to work – 'heart'.

"To handle yourself,
Use your head;
To handle others,
Use your heart!"

Author Unknown

Recognition versus Reward

Recognition and reward are often used synonymously or are combined into one system – the R & R system. These terms are very different and often the efforts to improve R & R systems totally neglect recognition. It is critical to clearly define these terms or you may fail to meet the employee satisfaction measure and quality of work life you are intending to attain.

As defined previously, recognition is acknowledgment, appreciation and approval. These elements, when combined and applied appropriately produce a psychological benefit – individuals have a sense of belonging and are intrinsically motivated.

Webster's New Collegiate Dictionary (G. & C. Merriam Co., 1981) defines *reward* in the following ways:

1. To give a reward to or for.
2. Recompense.
3. Something that is given in return for good or evil done or received and especially that is offered or given for a service.

Reward clearly indicates a financial benefit. Nothing in this definition indicates a psychological benefit. In fact, the definition reveals, as does history, that rewards can be gained for evil as well as good.

A survey and report by Carla O'Dell and Jerry McAdams, published by the American Productivity and Quality Center and the American Compensation Association revealed the following insights:

- A high 90.9% of respondents ranked 'recognition when I've done a job well' as Important or Very Important as a motivational factor. Surprisingly, it ranked above 'competitive salary' and 'pay clearly tied to performance' (rewards).
- Only 54.4% reported that their workplace provided this recognition.
- The median budget for recognition is $7-$23 an employee per year.
- Only 4-5% of the people in the companies surveyed received recognition. This is due to the fact that the recognition is set up for 'employee of the month',

'salesperson of the year', 'best service team'. These programs severely limit the number of people who qualify for recognition.

- Seventy-five percent of the respondents indicated subjective criteria such as 'management discretion', 'supervisory nomination', and 'superior performance event' was used to justify the decision to recognize.

Several conclusions can be drawn from these surveys. People want to be appreciated. Present work systems are not addressing this need. Receiving recognition is for the chosen few versus the vital many (everyone needs recognition). Most systems are subjective, competitive, demotivating to the majority who are 'losers', and management-driven.

W. Edwards Deming once stated:

"People are born with a need for relationships with other people, and with need to be loved and esteemed by others. There is innate need for self-esteem and respect. Management that denies to their employees dignity and self-esteem will smother intrinsic motivation."

Self-esteem, respect, intrinsic motivation and dignity are not guaranteed by a competitive salary.

Should recognition include a cash reward? In *People, Performance, and Pay* by Carla O'Dell in collaboration with Jerry McAdams, a summary of data collected on non-monetary awards versus cash showed: "There was approximately a 13% performance improvement using either non-monetary or cash awards. The cost of cash was nearly 12 cents for every dollar of increase. The cost of non-monetary awards was 4.1 cents for every dollar." Non-monetary awards clearly show a, "Significantly better return on investment." There is also a conclusion that in many situations non-monetary awards are more suitable than cash.

Of course, reward or compensation is very important, but having a very competitive compensation package does not eliminate the need for focus on recognition. The only way to ensure the appropriate level of concentration on recognition is to totally separate it from reward. Let's look at the differences.

Recognition	**Reward**
Non-cash	Monetary
Needed frequently	Infrequent changes
Psychological	Financial
Reinforces behaviors that can change corporate culture permanently; long-term changes	Supports short-term objectives, usually for the current quarter or year
Personal – from the 'heart'	Impersonal – from the 'wallet'
Value and principle-based	Based on corporate budget
Used to keep employees	Used to attract employees

The amount of time we invest in the workplace and our need to have positive interactions with others demands that recognition moves to the forefront of our work priorities. It can dramatically improve the quality of our work life. How often do we need to hear: "Another day, another dollar," or "I'm only here for the paycheck" before we go to work with our elaborate problem-solving processes to identify the root cause for this attitude? How many stress-related illnesses will we endure before we make creation of a good work environment a strategic priority by allowing people to care about each other and celebrate successes?

Just understanding the differences between reward and recognition may seem like a monumental task. There are some very simple solutions to this 'recognition versus reward' dilemma.

1. Never use 'reward' and 'recognition' in the same sentence.

2. Never have recognition and reward facilitated by the same person, team or functional group. Recognition requires people with psychological and motivational experience and expertise, while reward requires someone with financial, accounting and legal knowledge.

3. Keep cash for compensation; create a focus of sincere appreciation for recognition, and if combined with a tangible, make it a non-monetary award.

4. Train everyone in the importance of giving and receiving feedback in the workplace; do not limit this to a management responsibility.

5. Never give recognition based on a competition, lottery or subjective judgment; recognize all efforts that contribute to meeting your business vision, goals and objectives.

Some additional food for thought:

> *"It's easy to make a buck. It's a lot tougher to make a difference."*
>
> ***Tom Brokaw***

> *"What's the use you learning to do right, when it's troublesome to do right and ain't no trouble to do wrong, and the wages is just the same?"*
>
> ***The Adventures of Huckleberry Finn***
> ***Mark Twain***

What Recognition Isn't and What Isn't Recognition

When designing an effective recognition system, it is important not only to define what recognition is, but what approaches are not recognition.

Recognition isn't:

- *A competition.*

  Competition indicates a winner and losers. Everyone that makes a contribution toward the successful operation of the business, no matter how small, should be recognized and feel like a winner. If you only recognize or positively reinforce the 'sales person of the month' or the 'team of the year', then the majority of your work force has been left unappreciated. You should be able to say, "This year 100% of our work force received recognition! Every one of them made a valuable contribution." In most cases, less than 5% of the population are ever shown how the company appreciates their efforts.

- *A cash reward.*

  Cash is compensation – a reward. Recognition should focus on the sincere appreciation and thought, not the pocketbook. The majority of Americans live from paycheck to paycheck. Cash is definitely not a keepsake and the thought lasts about as long as it takes to spend the reward – for most of us, five minutes maximum!

- *A lottery.*

  Recognition should *never* be a game of chance or luck. One corporation provided each manager with a pair of tickets to a major sporting event to award as recognition to a deserving employee. Instead of spending some time, deciding who should receive the tickets and planning to present them in a thoughtful, well-planned manner, everyone's name was placed in a hat for a drawing. No specific behavior or practice was reinforced; the potential benefit was forfeited. In addition, a classic win/lose situation was created.

- *A quick, easy, low priority task.*

  It must be sincere, well-planned and properly executed. Do not take short cuts with one of the most valuable management tools in your possession! It takes time not only to identify those behaviors, practices and achievements critical to the success of your business, but to plan the appropriate recognition for each and how to deliver it in a meaningful, timely manner.

- *Boring.*

  Celebrate successes in a way meaningful to the recipient(s) and enjoyable for those being recognized. Nothing is worse than being invited to a stuffy awards ceremony or all-managers meeting. After accomplishing a quality improvement, there is a need for closure, the need to brag about and share what you have accomplished, the need to let your hair down and the need to gain the momentum required to undertake a new endeavor. Tom Peters has stated: "Celebrate what you want to see more of."

- *A scheduled activity.*

  "We will recognize one employee per quarter at the all managers meeting."

  This is definitely the wrong approach. Recognition should be spontaneous and timely. New habits do not develop overnight. So, until you integrate recognition into your daily activities, you may want to actually schedule time on your calendar at the end of your day to say 'thank you'. Always remember, the longer you wait to recognize the behavior, principle or practice, the less impact your reinforcement will have.

- *A replacement for compensation (and vice versa).*

  Both need to be used effectively and applied consistently and equitably. One without the other does not work. Remember, however that reward and recognition are not synonymous and address two entirely different needs. Providing a good salary to an employee will never replace their need to feel appreciated.

Take a moment to think about your current workplace practices that are called 'recognition'. If they do not meet the criteria for recognition including all three As (acknowledgment, appreciation, approval) and all seven characteristics for effective recognition (sincere, fair/consistent, timely, frequent, flexible, appropriate, specific), you will need to redesign your system. Here are some more examples of 'what isn't recognition'. Evaluate the following practices according to the seven characteristics for recognition and determine if they meet the qualifying criteria.

- *A raise in wages.*

  Salary raises are not frequent or timely. They are usually scheduled events and may follow months after an achievement. A cash exchange for a service is not appreciation, it is financial consideration in exchange for performance of designated tasks. It lacks the sincerity and warmth associated with a 'thanks'.

- *Giving stock options.*

  This also is a part of a compensation package. It does not meet the criteria of warm and sincere, immediate or flexible. Often, these stock options are given on the basis of length of service or position in the corporate hierarchy, neither of which reinforces any behavior other than 'being there' and 'being where'.

- *Improving the benefits package.*

  This is another compensation package feature given to everyone. It does not reinforce a specific practice or principle.

- *Something given to everyone – the turkey, free meal, holiday bonus, form letter . . .*

  These once a year or term vehicles are not frequent or sincere. You may save time in planning and execution, but you sacrifice the great benefits and gains associated with reinforcing a specific behavior or practice.

- *Anything forced or automatic; anything perceived as insincere.*

  Regularly scheduled vehicles such as service awards, which are not presented in a celebration environment lose their impact. Often, in large companies, these awards are distributed through the mail. Long-term service recognition should be accompanied with great fanfare. Any tool perceived as automatic sacrifices its intent.

- *A contest.*

  The word 'contest' suggests winners and losers. One company gave a presentation at a national conference about their recognition package which recognized 17 teams annually. When asked what the employee population was, the audience was told, "54,000." Then, they were asked how many teams the company had at present. The response was, "Hundreds." Not very good odds of being appreciated. Before you start a contest, you should think carefully. "Am I demotivating more people than I am motivating?" "Am I damaging teamwork?" We all have to deal with marketplace competition, which is stress enough. Keep the competition there, with the external forces. Internally, build bridges not walls. Your goal should be to make everyone successful, to have a company of winners not a handful.

Take the seven characteristics of effective recognition and measure your current recognition vehicles against these qualifications. You will probably see many opportunities for immediate improvement. It begins with your philosophy, principles and what you want to achieve. If you want to drive a culture change or implement a new method of conducting your business, make sure that you are not recognizing the wrong things, at the wrong time, with the wrong tool. If you want widespread change or implementation, make sure your tool recognizes a majority.

Chapter 2

The Recognition Process

"Practice an attitude of gratitude."

Author Unknown

Recognition Process

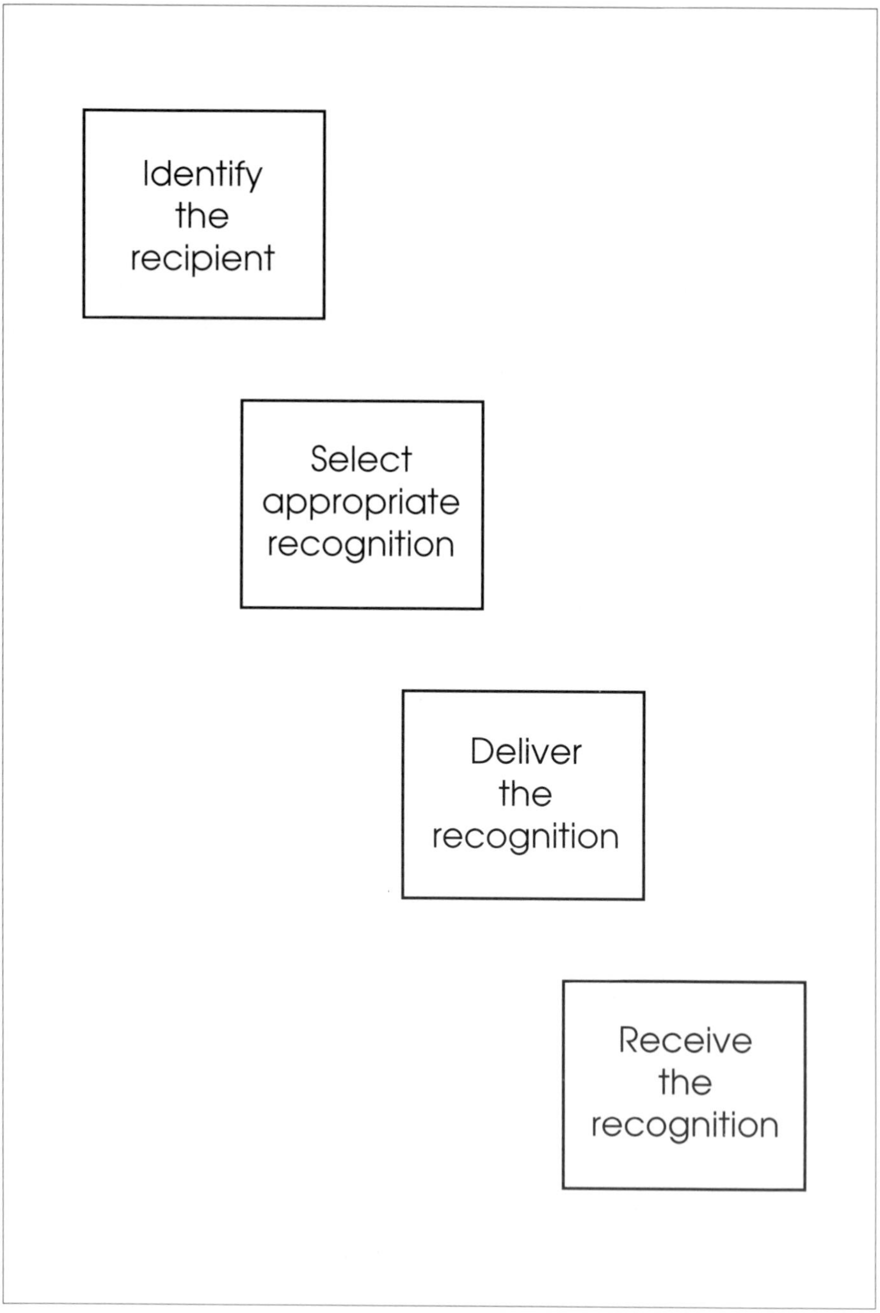

Identify the recipient

Select appropriate recognition

Deliver the recognition

Receive the recognition

Step One: Identifying the Recipient

Finding Opportunities to Recognize

Though the reality is all of us have bad work habits that are embarassing when held up for public review, we always find it more than a little amusing when someone asks, "When do I say thank you?" It happens at every presentation we have given. The answer is, "When you feel like it!" We get so caught up in the day-to-day performance of our assigned tasks, that we do not even notice the little things that our co-workers do to make it easier to do our jobs and to create a better work environment. As mentioned earlier, it is so much easier to identify the 'star' performer and major achievements and totally overlook the less obvious contributions and extra efforts exemplifying teamwork, quality improvement, creativity, innovation, leadership and initiative that enable the success of our teams, department and corporations on a daily basis. Every company is filled with 'behind the scenes' individuals who are busy contributing to the success of the whole.

The easiest way to develop this habit, as mentioned several times, is to schedule time at the end of each day for one week and challenge yourself to identify an individual or team that has made your work day a little nicer, your tasks a little easier, your processes a little better, your environment a little more organized or brighter, or even made you a little smarter. These individuals may not be 'stars', but they definitely have a positive impact on your effectiveness, productivity and/or attitude. We are sure, if you are truly committed to changing and improving your work and work life, you will find more opportunities than you will ever be able to address. Decide what behaviors or practices you want to see occur more frequently and recognize them. The results you achieve will be the behaviors, practices and principles you promote.

Let's look at some real-life scenarios of behaviors we reinforce that do not give us what we really want, but give us what we are asking for:

What we really want is high quality work to go to our customer.

In one department, an 'employee of the month' award is given for successfully completing 20 working days without having an error. This honor comes with $100 cash and a designated parking place. Carol has made it 19 days and six hours. Suddenly, a customer brings back an error. It really isn't Carol's fault, it was caused by faulty equipment. It is considered an 'error' as defined by the data collection procedure. The error measurements are self-collected. To make matters even more difficult, Carol just found out her daughter needs braces and she is going to have to come up with a $300 down payment. Several employees use this same piece of equipment and the problem causing the error will be identified eventually. Carol knows exactly what is wrong with the equipment as this same thing happened a year ago, but she needs the money and to get management to pay attention to the quality of her work.

What we really get is a normally honest employee seduced by money into a dishonest behavior and several more errors going to the customer before the problem is resolved.

What we really want is to meet corporate strategic goals.

Many corporations still have MBOs, the purpose of which is to recognize management fulfillment of their specific tasks and activities related to the corporate strategic goals. Once a year, the managers get cash bonuses, they go and purchase new clothes, new cars and take vacations. Their subordinates all watch as the second Christmas of the year happens for the elite class of the organization. If management is getting the reward, why should I do anything to improve? Why work hard when someone else is receiving the credit?

What we really get is 70-90% of the work force who don't care about the strategic goals, who don't focus on improving the processes related to achieving the goals, and who probably don't even know or care what the corporate strategic goals are. We could be reaching the goals quicker with more long-term solutions if we tapped the greatest resource – the people who perform the job, who make the difference.

What we really want is good teamwork and cooperation.

The majority of companies we have visited only have recognition tools in place for individual contributors, yet all of their training points to the obvious advantages of operating in a team. An employee has a great idea and could really use someone with experience in information systems and someone with a broader view of the business to ensure that any negative impact the idea might have on another functional process is addressed. The only recognition available is a 'trip for two' award and those awards are only given to individuals. There is no comparable team award. Should the employee ask management to put together a team and get the experts needed to fine-tune the idea, or go ahead and implement without this input to get the trip?

What we get are workers with ideas and methods that they guard like top secret Pentagon information. Many of these ideas are good, but lack the depth and experience that a team would bring to the final product. The practice of recognizing only individuals promotes the 'prima donna' approach. Equivalent individual and team recognition tools should be available to promote the multitude of efforts a business needs to be successful.

What we want are loyal employees.

Have you ever completed some monumental project and when someone at a high level in the corporate structure gives positive feedback, your manager or someone else steps up to take full credit? It has been said that the great leader is not the one in the spotlight, he's the one leading the applause, yet managers have not been recognized or rewarded for the number of their employees with great ideas. They are promoted on the basis of personal merit and achievement. Naturally, they take as much credit as possible.

What we get are demotivated employees who hold management in low regard.

What we want is the strength, effectivity and efficiency of a team.

One process improvement team solved a critical manufacturing problem, reducing the scrap rate and cycle time of a process. The manager took the whole team to lunch as a 'thank you'. Everything was going smoothly until the manager stood up at the end of the lunch and presented the team leader with a $100 gift certificate. As stated before, most company recognition programs and practices are designed for individual recognition, and even companies which have team recognition vehicles have erred by selecting an individual from a team to receive a higher level of recognition than the rest of the team members. This is *taboo!* As a general practice, all team members should be given the same level of recognition. Recognition for a 'most valuable player' on a team should only be given on an exception basis and only when driven by a spontaneous expression of the rest of the team.

What we get is everyone fighting to be the team leader and people unwilling to make contributions to the team if they are not the leader.

If you want these same behaviors and practices, keep with your old methods of operation. If you want to change the look of things, carefully consider what, who, where, when and how of your current recognition system and look for a different approach.

There are a great number of ways to recognize contributions in the workplace. When you think of personal experiences as a first level manager, do you remember feeling like you were between a rock and a hard place? Do you recall thinking, "What a thankless job! I am getting it from both ends, my subordinates and my superiors. I can't win?" And, what about being a supplier? Sometimes it feels like you could walk across water and your customer would then ask, "But, are you impervious to fire?" Your peers should be considered, too. Have you ever had those bad working relationship problems including:

- The peer whom you think is a friend, but whom you discover would steam roll over their own mother to look good themselves or to gain an edge.

- The peer who takes credit for your idea.
- The peer who sabotages your efforts because of a disagreement in approach.

Recognition tools and methods should be in place to make recognition possible in any direction – up and down the chain of command, across functions, internal and external to the company and among peers.

So often, your managers, fellow workers, suppliers and customers seem like traffic cops – the only time they pull you over is to tell you what you have done wrong. Is it any wonder we feel like we've been through the wringer by the time we get home at night? One good lesson to learn is to always look for the best in everyone, for everyone is special in some way. That is the key to finding opportunities to recognize. Instead of limiting our communication and efforts to finding what is wrong with everyone, we must refocus our attention on what is right with everyone. In addition, we must identify and positively reinforce what is 'goodness' for the business. Is it being a team player and cooperating, or is it being a solo act? Is it having the elite few concentrating on corporate strategies or having the entire employee population focused on critical business objectives? Is it operating with trust, credibility and respect or operating outside of these principles? First, change your communication focus and the way you look at others. Then, identify what is good for the business and begin to develop your plan for recognizing. You will have no problem finding the opportunities.

"The majority of us lead quiet, unheralded lives as we pass through this world. There will most likely be no ticker-tape parades for us, no monuments created in our honor. But that does not lessen our possible impact, for there are scores of people waiting for someone just like us to come along; people who will appreciate our compassion, our encouragement, who will need our unique talents. Someone who will live a happier life merely because we took the time to share what we had to give.

Too often we underestimate the power of a touch, a smile, a kind word, a listening ear, an honest compliment, or the smallest act of caring, all of which have the potential to turn a life around. It's overwhelming to consider the continuous opportunities there are to make our love felt."

Born for Love
Leo Buscaglia

What to Recognize

Activities and behaviors that deserve to be recognized cover a wide spectrum, from displaying an attitude that has a positive impact to completing projects with outstanding, measurable results. Remember, a 'state of the art' recognition system is flexible, accommodates a variety of different situations, and gives you the ability to say at the end of each year, "We recognized 100% of our employees this year!" Realize that any job well done is worth recognizing, and any behavior we appreciate and would like to see repeated is worth taking the time to say thank you. Some opportunities might include recognizing those:

- Having a positive impact on co-workers.
- Applying a process improvement tool effectively.
- Showing initiative.
- Displaying teamwork.
- Demonstrating extra effort.
- Exhibiting creativity.
- Identifying the solution to a recurring problem.
- Proposing an idea.
- Improving the work environment.

Try to realize that, in general, we have very high expectations of ourselves and others. It is important to avoid missing opportunities to say 'thanks'. If you are questioning, 'should I or shouldn't I', the answer is probably 'you should'!

Clearly define the purpose of recognition and then develop a list of behaviors and activities that support your corporate mission. For instance, the purpose of recognition from page 2 is:

> *"To acknowledge and appreciate those behaviors and practices that establish a working environment that promotes the concepts of loyalty, belonging, confidence, self-worth, teamwork, respect, creativity and trust through frequent and sincere methods of approval."*

What behaviors and practices support your business objectives and goals? Do these support your recognition mission? At one location, the following list was created:

Behaviors	**Practices**
Time sacrifice	Impact on department goal
Extra effort	Impact on organizational goal
Excellence in daily work	Impact on company goal
Willing to volunteer	Customer focus
Caring and respectful	Risk taking
Consistently positive and approachable	Solving a product performance problem
Supportive	Exemplary leadership
Honest	Revenue improvement

These are not the complete lists, but will give you an idea of how you should proceed. Whatever qualities are important to the success of your endeavor, whether it is a desired behavior, method of operation or impact to a goal, you must ensure that you have an easy method to facilitate immediate recognition for the contribution.

Who is Responsible for Recognition?

Make recognition the responsibility of *everyone* in the workplace. Design the processes so that anyone can initiate the recognition and anyone can receive the recognition. Develop guidelines and training for all employees. If you limit the recognition responsibility to the management team, the results you get will be the results you have always had. It is unfair to the management, unfair to the people and unfair to the company which loses the benefits, which potentially include a highly focused and positive work force.

The main argument against an employee-driven system involves a lack of trust. 'They will spend too much money'! 'They won't get their work done'. I assure you, with the proper amount of forethought and time spent in developing and piloting your system, you can build integrity into your programs. Most of the time, you will be surprised at how people can act responsibly when given the authority of being empowered and entrusted with obligations.

In the next section, you will see examples of employee-driven tools and techniques that have proven to be successful.

Step Two: Selecting the Appropriate Recognition

Considerations When Selecting a Recognition Vehicle

The opportunities to recognize are limitless, as are the results you will see. Create a toolbox of recognition vehicles, so that you will have a method available for every situation. It wouldn't make sense to recognize a team who had realized a saving of $500,000 annually by improving their process with the same recognition vehicle you give an individual for reorganizing a file cabinet. And, you definitely do not want to tie recognition with a dollar amount or return-on-investment, for there are several intangible efforts that cannot be measured, but may be equally important to the organization. As stated repeatedly, effective recognition is not an easy or quick task. There are several considerations, but the two most important are:

- *What is being recognized?*

  The type of recognition selected should be proportionate to the activity. If the activity represents a significant accomplishment and the recognition is perceived as insignificant, its effect could be extremely demotivating. On the other hand, a tremendous acknowledgment for a small accomplishment not only seems insincere and inappropriate, it creates a false expectation of the same in the future.

- *What type of recognition would be valued by the recipient?*

  The personal touch is the most important aspect of recognition. Knowing what the recipient values is a major part of the decision. Someone in an office environment may appreciate a certificate, wall plaque or desk accessory, while someone working in a clean room environment would have no place to display this type of recognition.

You can develop several types of recognition vehicles, suitable to either individual recognition or team recognition. Determining the appropriate vehicle is very important. The type of recognition selected must match the level of accomplishment or behavior achieved. As the significance of the contribution increases, so should the type of recognition. The following matrix shows how the different types of recognition levels were developed at one company and provides examples of matching the appropriate level of recognition to the level of accomplishment.

Recognition Categories

Level One	Level Two
Action Required: • Significant personal impact.	**Action Required:** • Significant impact on department/organizational/ corporate goal.
Award Value: • Up to $10.	**Award Value:** • Up to $100.
Examples: Demonstration of quality behaviors shown by: • Time sacrifice. • Extra effort. • Teamwork. • Participation. • Excellence in daily work. • Volunteering. • Positive attitude. • Caring/respectful. • Supportive. • Follow-through. • Improvement to quality of work life or safety. • Improvement to non-critical work processes.	**Examples:** Demonstration of quality principles and practices shown by: • Focus on customer requirements. • Achieving departmental, functional or organizational goal. • Leadership by example. • Innovation/risk taking. • Successful application of problem-solving or quality improvement methods by an individual, cross-functional team or department team to key processes in their area.
Types of Awards: • Thanks. • Tokens. • Merchandise.	**Types of Awards:** • Merchandise. • Team Excellence celebrations. • Night on the Town. • 'I Made a Difference' award.

Although management involvement in approval is sometimes required, this system is not management-driven. *Anyone can initiate* any vehicle, making this an employee-driven recognition system. In addition, the matrix provides some guidelines, so that recognition tools are used consistently and responsibly. The important thing to note is that every possible type of contribution is covered from a personal behavior to a corporate contribution. If one category is inappropriate, another one is suitable. Instead of management saying 'no' to a recognition opportunity, if the award suggested seems excessive they have the ability to suggest an alternative. *Everyone gets recognized*. The matrix only goes to an award of $100 in value; we feel that any contribution meriting greater attention should be recognized with an award *and* rewarded with a compensation increase. By exceeding a certain perceived value, the recognition will become compensation. The following sections will provide you with ideas for recognition vehicles to satisfy personal impact, and significant departmental, organizational or corporate contributions.

Tools for Recognizing Personal Impact – Level One

As shown on the Recognition Categories matrix, the features of the Level One tools for recognizing significant personal impact include:

- There is no management approval required.
- The awards have perceived values of less than $10; they are simply tokens of appreciation.
- The recognition is appropriate for anyone and for any work-related behavior that is deemed helpful or exemplary of good working practices, principles or habits.
- Although this tool is labeled as 'peer-to-peer', you can use it for anyone – a subordinate, superior, supplier, customer, industry associate or peer.

It is important that these Level One vehicles meet the criteria established by the purpose of recognition, the definition of recognition and the seven characteristics of recognition. Also, they should be immediate, simple to use and readily available. Some examples of 'personal impact' recognition vehicles and processes are as follows:

Thank You Cards

Thank you cards are an effective way to tell others how we appreciate something they have done for us. We use them in our personal lives and they can be used just as effectively as a person-to-person method of recognition in the workplace. The beauty of the 'thank you' is that it is simple, spontaneous, immediate and can be used to recognize anyone – customer, supplier, peer, subordinate or superior. It is not a method that requires management approval.

Design an attractive thank you card using high quality stationery and colorful graphics, and include the company or organizational logo with a blank space inside for a handwritten message. Make it something that individuals will be proud to display in their offices. Add a matching envelope to make it a vehicle for external as well as internal use. Thank you notes should be placed in locations convenient to all employees, where it takes no longer than a minute to retrieve it. Encourage the giver to take the thank you note and personally present it to the recipient when possible, further reinforcing the behavior or practice.

The following are a few examples of behaviors and attributes that might be recognized with this method:

- Caring/respectful.
- Displaying creativity/innovation.
- Showing customer-orientation.
- Putting forth extra effort.
- Displaying a quality orientation.
- Flexibility.

- Providing assistance/supportive.
- Volunteering.
- Exhibiting initiative.
- Exhibiting leadership.
- Actively participating.
- Positive attitude.
- Approachable.
- Taking a risk.
- Being a team player.
- Making a time sacrifice.
- Serving as an idea-generator.
- Demonstrating resourcefulness.

Does this method seem a little too simple to be called recognition? Let's see if it fits our criteria?

✔ The definition of recognition.

Appreciation – it is a thank you note. Acknowledgment – the message states why I am thanking the individual; my name and the recipient's name have been personally handwritten, as well as the behavior or practice. Approval – I liked what the recipient did so well that I took time to personally write the message and personally deliver it.

✔ The purpose of recognition.

"To acknowledge and appreciate those behaviors and practices that establish a working environment that promotes the concepts of loyalty, belonging, confidence, self-worth, teamwork, respect, creativity and trust through frequent and sincere methods of approval." If I have thanked a peer for helping me proof a document, I have reinforced the concept that teamwork makes a better product, and the individual's worth to me by noting their skills, talents and willingness to help that I appreciate.

✔ The characteristics of recognition.

1. Sincere – the message is from the heart not the pocketbook or a copying machine.
2. Fair and consistent – everyone is included and any work-related behavior or practice that a person values can be recognized.
3. Timely – it is immediate.
4. Frequent – you can write or receive as many 'thank yous' as warranted.
5. Flexible – it can fit any internal or external situation.
6. Appropriate – there is never a situation when a 'thank you' or sincere appreciation is inappropriate. In fact, no matter what is being appreciated or what token of appreciation you are using, it should be required.
7. Specific – the behavior or practice is handwritten in the card.

The process addresses all the criteria, requires little training and can be implemented easily. This is a good starting point for your new philosophy and policy on recognition.

One of the vice presidents in a corporation where a 'thanks system' was implemented stated during the presentation for management approval of the system: "This is too corny! I guess we can try it, since this team is convinced that it will help." One month after implementation, he received his first thank you card and came running out of his office to show it to everyone close by. Anyone witnessing this event would have thought he had just won the state lottery. He carefully mounted the card on his wall to display. Today, there are several thank you cards which have joined that first message, and he can proudly boast that he is the VP with the most. They remain on his wall and are a constant reminder to him of what is important – a sort of living memorial to his management style and being people-oriented. Management used to be a thankless job or maybe people did appreciate certain things and qualities, but did not have the vehicle to express themselves.

Tokens

Tokens are 'funny money'. There are several novelty manufacturers which will produce your coins or currency. One example of a company token has 'Thanks' and the logo of the recognition system on one side, and the corporate policy statement on the other. In addition, small cardboard token holders were purchased to hold the token, carrying a description of the exchange options. The token can be any nominal amount. You can make it exchangeable in any way(s) you want. They can be accumulated for higher awards, much like carnival tickets with points that you collect for prizes. If your corporation is large, you can bring attention to other internal corporate businesses. Here's an example of one method of setting up a token system.

Tokens may be redeemed for $3 a piece in the following places:

- *Company Logo Merchandise Catalog.*

  All catalog items carry the corporate logo, so company pride is promoted (an added benefit).

- *Employee Recreation Association.*

  The recreation association has movie tickets, tickets to sporting events and concerts, as well as various clubs with membership fees. The recipient may share recognition with family members.

- *Wellness Center.*

  The wellness center offers classes in exercise, smoking cessation and diet management. This encourages people to use these services which make for a healthier employee.

- *Company Cafeteria.*

  The cafeteria is convenient and used by almost all employees. There is no change given for tokens as they are not really cash.

- *Gift Certificates.*

  Several types of gift certificates have been made available such as coupons to pizza parlors, book stores, merchandise, discount and department stores, car washes, restaurants, etc. This provides a variety of options that will fit any individual's needs.

Due to the fact that tokens have a perceived value, certain measures and monitoring must take place including:

1. Require that only one token may be given per thank you.

2. Tokens must always be accompanied by a personal thank you card.

3. Set up a network of coordinators with sign out sheets for tokens; have an administrator to monitor token usage.

4. Never allow cash to be exchanged, either straight across or for change.

Here is one company's process for using a 'Thanks Process' with a thank you card and token.

Example of Level One Recognition Process

'Thanks Process' with Token Option

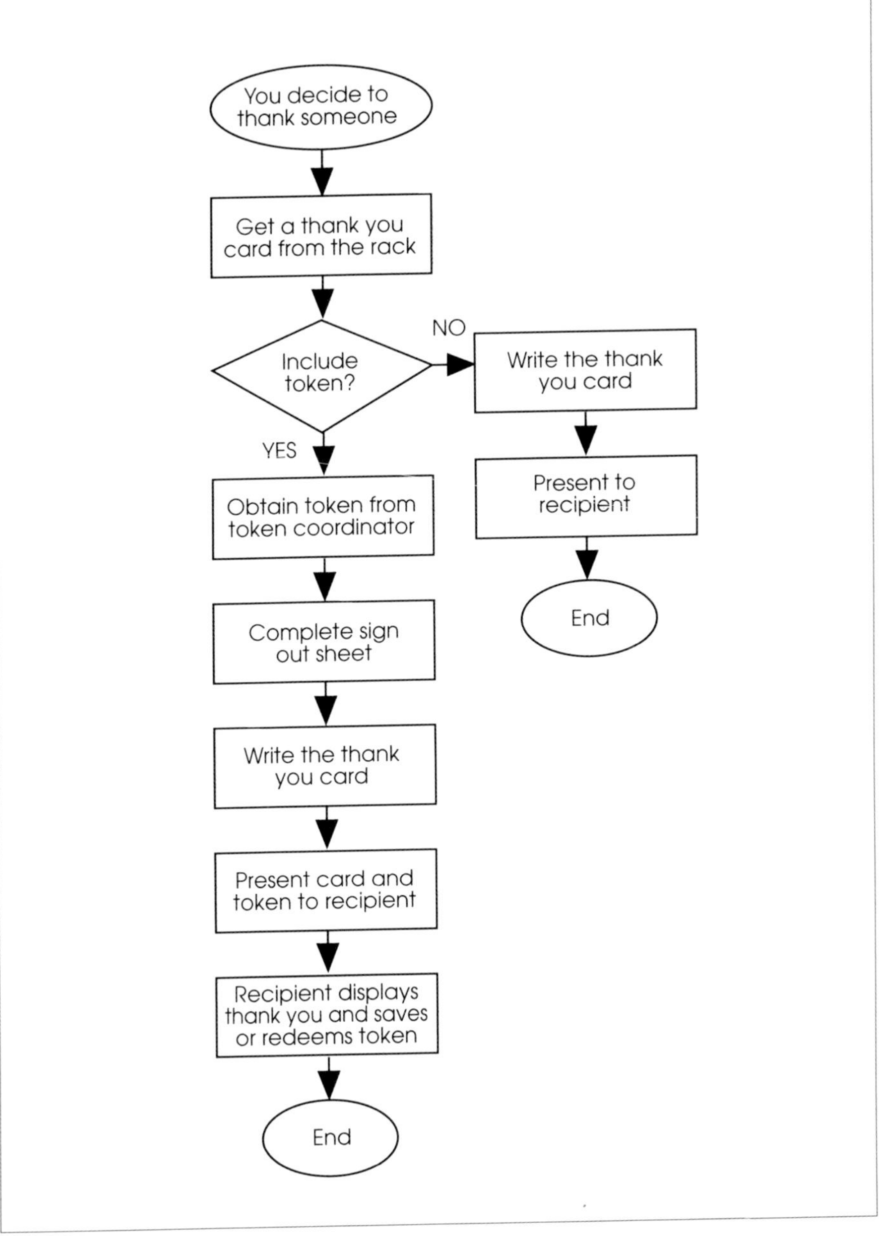

We have observed tokens used in other situations including:

- *Hotel.*

  The hotel asked each customer to fill out an input card on the different services the hotel offered (maid service, valet parking, check-in/check out desk, room service, bell service, etc.). If the highest rating was achieved, the group received a token to be accumulated for a team party. The purpose of this system was to ensure the best customer service possible.

- *A Major Appliance Store.*

  The store solicited customer feedback on sales and service representatives during a follow-up phone call to customers. Any employee who received praise from the customer received a token. Tokens could be saved toward the purchase of anything in the store.

Gifts or Gift Certificates

A gift to thank someone for a positive behavior is a regular activity in our personal lives and can easily be a work practice. Special merchandise can be ordered specific to your team effort, department, product, organization or corporation. These gifts might include a special coffee mug, T-shirt, or hat that notes the special activity. These gifts serve as a constant reminder, a keepsake of what the individual or team did to receive the recognition.

Pizza Party or Barbecue

This is an easy and relatively simple way to reinforce a small group for accomplishing something which may not have been a specific department goal, but which positively affected everyone in the department – such as a new way to organize the area that makes it easier to retrieve information or putting plants in the area to brighten the work atmosphere. It is relatively inexpensive, but, when combined with sincere appreciation from the beneficiaries of the effort and a mini-celebration, is effective recognition.

Wall of Fame

Buy a few inexpensive cameras, some bulletin boards and distribute them throughout the company. Give the cameras to designated 'photographers', who become responsible for taking pictures of individuals and teams who have exemplified the principles and practices defined by the business goals during the last month. Place the pictures and a brief description of the activities on the bulletin board to showcase for the next month. Accomplishments are visible to everyone and the individuals in the showcase become role models and are reinforced again for their contributions.

Other Level One Recognition Ideas

- Take an advertisement out in the local newspaper thanking the team members for their success (list each individual's name).
- Award movie tickets.
- Take the team to breakfast.

Just ensure that either a thank you card or a show of sincere appreciation is included with these forms of recognition.

Tools for Recognizing Significant Department, Organizational and Corporate Impact – Level Two

Tools for recognizing significant department impact are noted as Level Two recognition on the Recognition Categories matrix on page 30. This is a higher level of recognition which includes a non-monetary award with a perceived value of $15 to $100. A Level Two recognition award is given for participating in an effort that had a significant impact on a business goal, or in the case of a cross-functional effort, a Level Two recognition award would be for an improvement that yielded a significant impact on cycle time, costs or quality of a product or service. This type of recognition does require first level management approval. There are two important things to remember for processes requiring management approval:

1. Always make the nomination process simple and available to everyone.
2. Management should never have to say 'no'.

To accomplish these two objectives, ensure that there is a simple nomination form that spells out the requirements, so that when an individual or team is seeking recognition, it is clear. Train managers in the different recognition tools, so if a nomination does not merit a certain level of recognition, they can offer some reasonable alternatives to the nominator, provide everyone with a procedure which supports the decisions.

Here is an example of a form that meets the requirements. It clearly spells out the requirements for a Level Two recognition, yet leaves the signing manager with an alternative of different levels at the end.

Level Two Team Nomination Form

Mail to:
Process Administrator

All information in this package must be completed. Thank you!

Team Name ____________________ Date of Application ____________________

Team Member Information

Name	Div/Dept	MS	EXT.	Manager	MS	EXT.

*Any additional members may be listed on a separate sheet attached to this form.

Contact Person ____________________ MS ____________ Extension ____________

Please complete all three pages of this form

Problem/Mission Statement

Brief description of team's accomplishment

Show desired measurable results

Please complete all three pages of this form

Sponsor Section

(To be completed by the team's sponsoring manager)

☐ Application is complete; all sections have been completed and measurable results provided.

Select One. The appropriate level of recognition for this team is:

☐ **Level One**

This team addressed issues affecting personal/individual roles and responsibilities in the workplace. Some examples include: time sacrifice, extra effort in a specific situation, improving the organization of the work area to better facilitate task accomplishment, improving team dynamics, etc.

or

This team addressed a process improvement opportunity or problem other than those identified as a key business process in the department or organization.

☐ **Level Two – Team Excellence Celebration and Award**

☐ **Level Two – Night on the Town Award**

☐ **Level Two – 'I Made a Difference' Award**

This team completed a process improvement or made a significant contribution toward meeting or exceeding a department/organizational/corporate strategic goal established for a key business process. Measurable results demonstrate impact on the goals stated for the key business process. For example, reduced cycle time, reduced scrap costs or improved inventory turns.

Signature of Sponsor ________________________________

My signature verifies that this team has satisfied the minimum requirement for the level of award selected.

Please complete all three pages of this form

Some examples of Level Two recognition processes follow.

Team Excellence Celebration and Award

The Team Excellence Celebration and Award provides a means to recognize teams for their successes. As you can see by the preceding form, Team Excellence requires a completed team nomination form, the team mission statement, evidence of measurable results, and the signature of the process owner (beneficiary of the improvement). The features of this kind of team recognition are the following: anyone can initiate it, the process is simple, and the nominees receive positive reinforcement in three ways. This award is designed for celebration and takes into consideration the importance of recognition from family, peers and management. It is a three-tiered recognition:

1. The immediate recognition is given by the process owner. It includes a certificate identifying the specific contribution, a lapel pin recognizing Team Excellence and a sincere verbal thank you.

2. The team is invited to a *celebration*, not to be confused with a banquet, a luncheon, or an award ceremony. Each individual is allowed to bring one guest. This guest can be a co-worker, friend, family member – anyone the recipient chooses.

3. Each individual team member is allowed to select one award item from a list of 8-10 logo items, such as binoculars, garment bag, jacket, desk clock, etc. The Team Excellence logo notes that they have actively participated in a successful team effort. These items are not for sale anywhere and can only be obtained through this achievement.

Some examples of measurable results might include:

- Reduction in cycle time.

- Reduction in defect rate.
- Reduction in quality costs.
- Development of a new process or new product.
- Return on investment.
- Reliability improvement.
- Cost reduction or avoidance.
- Reduction in labor hours.
- Increase in customer or employee satisfaction indices.

Here is how the process works:

Team Excellence Process

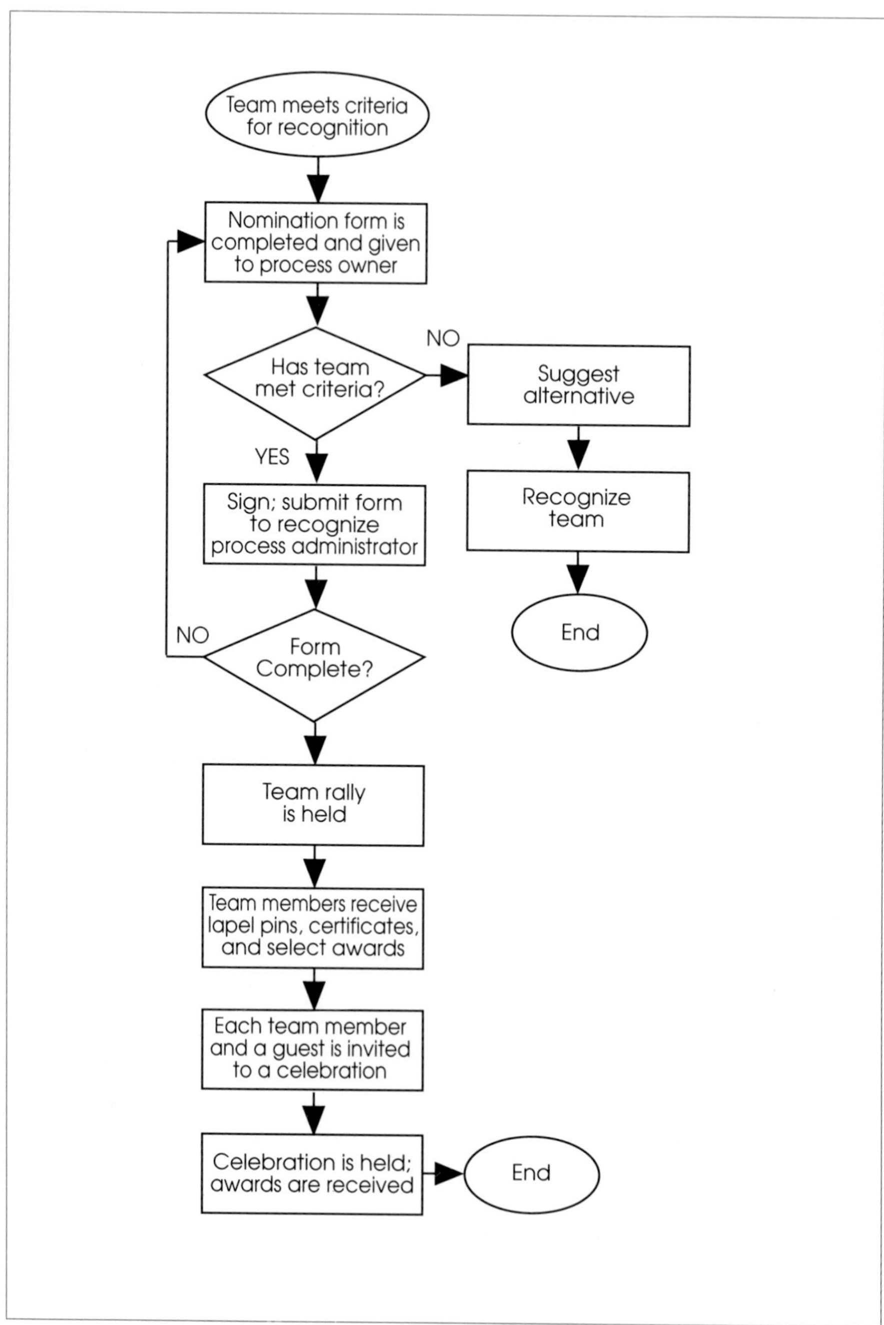

Let's talk about *celebration!* The celebrations are not your typical award ceremonies which are stuffy and often overly formalized. They are held during work hours. They happen frequently during the year. They are limited to four or five teams per celebration to keep them small and personal. And most importantly, they are theme celebrations designed for fun! Use your imagination! Here are two examples of celebrations:

Celebration #1 – The Oscars.

Clever and appropriately designed invitations are mailed announcing the theme. Of course, all participants are fed, but in addition, the room is decorated with top hats, glitter and chocolate champagne bottles. Everyone in attendance knows in advance of the theme and may dress to suit the occasion. Some show up in 'tux-look-alike' T-shirts and boas. All of a sudden, the lights dim, the music starts and spotlights move rapidly across the audience. Jodie Foster and Hannibal the Cannibal (a man on a dolly in restraining mask and straight jacket) impostors walk (or roll) in to host the event. At this event, each team was allowed to nominate a person that wasn't a team member but served as a vital support person during the project. These individuals have their accomplishments cited and are called forward to receive chocolate Oscars for 'Best Supporting Actor or Actress'. A team game is played in which each table tries to match the actors or actresses with the Academy Award winning film. The first team with a correct entry, gets chocolate champagne bottles. As participants enjoy their meal, Academy Award winning music is played over the sound system. Each team has a designated speaker who gives a five-minute informal presentation on what the team accomplished and introduces each team member. At this time, they are thanked by a director or VP of their organization and given the award they selected previously. A guest speaker gives a five-minute presentation encouraging the team members to continue their good work.

Celebration #2 – The Fabulous Fifties.

This event follows the same agenda as Celebration #1, but saddle shoes, mouse ears and poodle skirts are the dress. Two Elvis impersonators entertain the crowd (both are employees of the company). The decorations are 45 records, soda glasses, jukeboxes, 1950s model cars, etc. During lunch, the tunes of Connie Francis, Brenda Lee, Buddy Holly and other 1950s stars are played. Any individual who can produce a credit card, check, employee number or any document with the numbers 1950 in series receives a video tape rewinder that looks like a model '57 Chevy. Each table team is asked to reach consensus and guess the number of gum balls in a gum ball machine. The winning team gets 1950s memorabilia. The team's designated speakers get officially inducted into the Mickey Mouse club and receive their ears. And so on . . .

The only standard items on the Team Excellence Celebration agenda are the team five-minute presentations, the guest speaker and a meal. From there, you can expect almost anything, making the event fun, exciting, always surprising – a *celebration* of success! Some other themes and highlights of Team Excellence Celebrations include:

- Luau – hula-hoop competition and name that Hawaiian tune.

- Olympics – game winners won gold medals (chocolate), were put on a pedestal and had the flag raised behind them to the National Anthem. An opening torch was lit. The team game was naming the countries of the flags decorating the walls.

- Fiesta – Mariachis played. Sombreros with flowers decorated the tables. Carmen Miranda hosted the event. The team game was identifying the prices of fast food items from Taco Bell™ – 59, 79 or 99.

There are hundreds of ideas to make the event an experience to remember.

The awards for the recipients are of a perceived value of $75-$100 and are changed frequently to provide a variety. All have the Team Excellence logo to remind the recipient every time he/she looks at the item of their achievement. Some examples of awards are binoculars, sweatshirts, jackets, garment bags, locker bags, data banks for personal information, oak desk sets, etc. There should always be a continuously changing inventory to ensure that recipient needs are met. The most popular items may be kept for a longer time period.

If you are trying to promote the team approach to work, this is a perfect recognition tool.

Night on the Town Awards

Another form of Level Two recognition is The Night on the Town. The Night on the Town is a type of recognition that provides an opportunity for employees to celebrate their exemplary work achievements with family and/or friends. It may be used to recognize an individual or a team. The immediate recognition is an attractive certificate noting the achievement which may be displayed. Again, anyone can nominate any individual or team for this award. The criteria is basically the same as those for Team Excellence. Certificates can be made available throughout the company. To make it valid for exchange, the process owner must sign the certificate and indicate their division/department number. The stub on the certificate may be exchanged in two ways:

1. For a $100 gift certificate at a local fancy dining establishment.
2. For $140 of $10 denomination certificates good at several local fast food restaurants and reasonably priced family restaurants.

This type of recognition is valuable to use for individual recognition and in those cases where a Team Excellence celebration is not the choice of the recipients. Like the celebration, it allows the recipient the opportunity to share their work success with family and friends.

The 'I Made a Difference' Award

This type of recognition is provided for the same type of contribution required by Team Excellence or the Night on the Town criteria. It is offered to those teams and individuals that might prefer a shopping spree and includes three options for gift certificates at local department stores or through a catalog. The process for initiation and redemption is the same as for a Night on the Town.

Significant Contribution Award Process

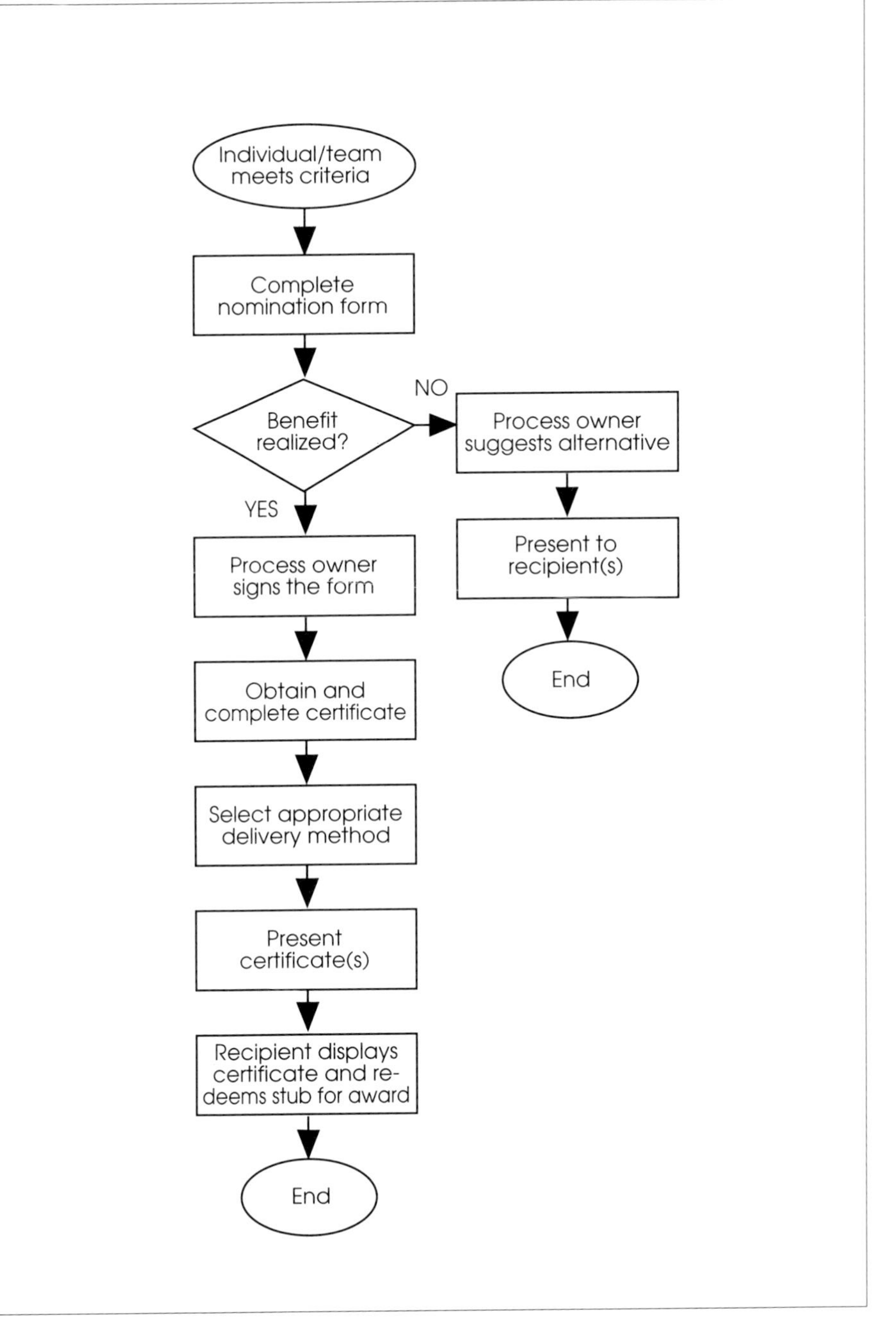

Other Types of Level Two Recognition

- Day off with pay.
- Taking a team to lunch and a baseball game.
- Providing chauffeur service to and from work for a day.
- Group planned event.

Any of these examples are fine as long as they stay within the value guidelines ($15-$100) and include a show of sincere appreciation, acknowledgment and approval.

Step Three: Delivering the Recognition

Guidelines for Giving

Nothing is more enjoyable than giving someone a gift or making someone feel special. It is equally rewarding for the giver and the recipient. Remember the seven criteria for effective recognition when delivering the recognition:

1. *Be sincere.*

   Nothing is worse than receiving appreciation or a gift from someone who really doesn't care. Use your words, your body language and your token of appreciation to express *real* gratitude.

2. *Be fair and consistent.*

   Inequitable, inconsistent or excessive recognition may be perceived as an insult, negating the positive results you want to achieve.

3. *Be timely.*

   An historical failure with recognition systems is that the recipient had to wait a year to receive recognition and the recognition process was weighed down with competitions, scoring and mounds of administration. The tools suggested previously provide for immediate recognition and the more immediate the recognition, the more likely you are to see the behavior or practice repeated.

4. *Recognize frequently.*

   Recognition should occur as often as the behaviors or practices are demonstrated. The Thanks system mentioned earlier can be applied liberally. Remember, the goal is to have recognition for everyone and to improve the quality of our work life. This goal requires that recognition become part of our daily thoughts and work activity.

5. *Be flexible.*

   Spontaneous recognition should become the norm. The recognition processes in this book take very little time to initiate and allow for not only spontaneity, but creativity in making the recognition a personal statement from the giver.

6. *Ensure the recognition is appropriate.*

   Do not just recognize so often that the positive results of recognition are lost in the flurry of activity. Lay out a plan, defining what behaviors and practices are valuable to your business and how you plan to show appreciation on the occasions where the opportunity arises. Do not recognize at random.

7. *Be specific.*

   Let the recipient know exactly what you are recognizing and chances are history will repeat itself.

Types of Acknowledgment

There are many ways to acknowledge contributions. Remember, always consider the feelings of the recipient. Secondly, recognize with a method that is comfortable to you, so the message received is sincere, warm and heartfelt.

Let's look at the types of acknowledgment.

Public or Private Acknowledgment

Public recognition should always be considered as the delivery method of choice as there is increased motivational value to both the receiver and the audience when attention is called to specific behaviors and practices. Public recognition has a much greater impact than recognition given privately.

If the receiver is particularly shy, embarrassed easily or very private, the giver should take into account these feelings and deliver the recognition with little or no fanfare. Private recognition may also be the delivery of choice when public recognition would elicit feelings of favoritism or undue competitiveness.

The decision to give public or private recognition requires knowing the recipient, the recipient's peer environment and the presenter's own comfort level. As recognition becomes the rule instead of the exception in your workplace, public recognition should progress to where it is the norm and the chosen method of delivery accepted by everyone as a positive experience.

Formal or Informal Recognition

This decision is usually based on the magnitude of the accomplishment. In situations where the achievement commands considerable attention, the ceremonial quality and visibility afforded by formal recognition tends to be more appropriate. Again, some individuals may be very uncomfortable in a formal setting and their feelings should be considered. Recognition is evolving into the art of celebration, having fun and being in a comfortable situation.

Verbal and/or Written Recognition

A one-on-one verbal acknowledgment of a positive behavior or an exceptional accomplishment is the foundation to any recognition.

When the behavior or accomplishment mainly affects the two parties, a sincere personal expression of acknowledgment and appreciation is the most appropriate. Prior to recognizing an individual or team in a peer environment, personal verbal recognition can ensure the proper amount of time is spent communicating the specific reason for the recognition to the recipient. There are several ways to facilitate verbal acknowledgment in the work place including staff meetings, special meetings and an informal calling-together of the peer group.

The appropriate way to decide how the verbal recognition will be given is by determining what audience would most benefit from hearing about the behavior or accomplishment. The recognition never should be given as an aside during a meeting. It should command special attention and include a statement of what the candidate did, why you consider it special and noteworthy, and how the activity helps the audience.

Documenting the recognition with a simple thank you or a more formal memo is a way to reemphasize what you have shared verbally. It allows the giver to be personal and warm, and records the event to serve as a reminder or keepsake for the recipient. The document also allows the recipient to share the recognition with family, friends and co-workers. Written recognition can take many forms including a thank you note, a letter of commendation or an article in the company news. It is critical to remember, there is little or no value in a form letter with a stamped signature!

Double the Value

The most valuable delivery method is to recognize using a verbal method reinforced with a written document, which is possible regardless of the formality or public or private setting.

Step Four: Receiving the Recognition

For some reason, our culture has conditioned us to deny or minimize compliments immediately. For instance, if someone says, "I love your dress!" you automatically reply with a denial, "This old thing? I gave 10 bucks for it at a garage sale!" Or maybe you say, "Gosh, I hardly ever wear it because I think it over-emphasizes my hips!" Never is the compliment accepted at face value or affirmed by saying, "It is one of my favorites, too." We all need to learn to accept praise unconditionally and graciously. The act of recognizing takes a great deal of forethought and work. It is coming from the heart of the giver and often the recognition exchange is as important, valuable and exciting to the giver as it is to the receiver. Train yourself to be receptive to the giver and enjoy the benefits of feeling better about yourself and your work.

Be happy and celebrate!

Chapter 3

Implementation Strategies

"Treat people as they are, and they remain that way. Treat them as though they were what they can be, and we can help them become what they are capable of becoming."

Goethe

"If it is to be, it is up to me."

William H. Johnsen

Evolution versus Revolution

People do not like to have the 'rug jerked out from under them'. Change is difficult, even for the most progressive. If you are revising your current recognition system, try an evolutionary approach. Plan the change with ease of acceptance in mind. Our evolutionary plan included the following strategies and tactics:

1. *Keep your current recognition tools as you introduce the new ones.*

   Even though the former recognition tools, $50 and $100 cash certificates, did not meet our criteria for effective recognition, we continued to provide these awards. By doing this, we avoided the perception that something was being taken away. These old systems of recognition, over a period of three years, significantly decreased from lack of interest and usage. As people became familiar with the new tools, which included the 'caring and sharing' and more personal touches, they became the tools of choice.

2. *Pilot the tools one at a time in a small section of your corporation.*

   We piloted our thanks cards combined with tokens in an organization of 1800 people, approximately 20% of the corporate population. We followed with the Team Excellence celebrations and the Night on the Town recognition processes. In this way, we started with the needs of the majority first. 'Thanks' was only in place for three months when other organizations began requesting participation. By conducting pilots, you can collect data on costs and employee satisfaction to provide to those organizations less likely to take a risk without more information. This also provides the opportunity to fine tune the system before wider deployment.

3. *Measure each tool for employee satisfaction and make improvements continuously.*

   Many of our measurements are collected in-process. For example, surveys collected from a random sample of Team Excellence participants have results plotted on a control chart. One control chart showed the rating on the meal went 'out of control' after one celebration. The menu was changed before the next celebration bringing our process back into control. By monitoring eight different attributes of the celebration process, we can stay on top of recipient needs.

4. *Charter a cross-functional team to select awards, roll-out new tools, track and improve processes, and plan Team Excellence celebrations.*

   A management assumption during our development phase was that engineers, assemblers, managers, consultants, accountants and administrative associates would not all respond to the same recognition tool. We have no hard data to support this assumption. Everyone likes to feel appreciated and the gift is definitely not the focus. In order to address this concern, we created a cross-functional recognition council. This council functions as a steering committee and has one representative from each functional organization.

5. *Ensure that management is well-versed in the recognition philosophy and tools.*

   We began by giving management overviews. Whenever you empower people and give them new responsibilities, it is critical to train them for the 'handing over the baton'. To encourage the entire work force to accept this new responsibility, we asked the managers to serve as role models and actively participate in the recognition processes. We also gained their agreement to guide their reports in proper usage of the tools.

6. *Produce and distribute a procedure manual to every employee.*

   All recognition methods had process flow charts and accompanying procedures. It was critical that recognition be considered a work process, no different than any other work process. This manual helped reinforce the fact that recognition was not an 'extra' or a 'nice gesture'. Each recognition process was continuously improved using the corporation's standardized quality improvement process. By distributing to every employee, we reinforced the concept that recognition is everyone's responsibility.

7. *Select a high-level sponsor.*

   It is critical to find a true believer in the upper layers of management who will run interference for your efforts and secure the necessary resources. At one point, we almost lost part of our system due to a budget cut. Our sponsor prevented this catastrophe. In addition, he hired a full-time recognition process administrator to maintain the system. This further validated the importance of recognition in the workplace. Oddly enough, our sponsor was the vice-president of manufacturing, not the person or function you would guess would take responsibility for these processes. This turned out to be a blessing in disguise. It was the largest organization, placing the recognition support where it would be the most visible. It was isolated from the 'reward' function, so recognition finally gained the focus it rightfully deserved. Finally, it kept recognition out of the corporate bureaucracy that might threaten the simplicity and availability of the tools. It was a total paradigm shift and a major risk that paid off for all functional organizations. Only through the belief and people-oriented management style of our sponsor, did the system achieve its full potential.

8. *Establish a recognition network.*

Walt Disney once said: "Many hands, hearts and minds generally contribute to anyone's notable achievements." One person could not make any of these processes work. Not even 10 people could. We began by soliciting one volunteer from each department to work on recognition. We gave each individual special holders for thank you's, a supply of thank you cards and envelopes, and 50 tokens. We explained the importance of their role in starting and maintaining the process. We followed with regular one-on-one communication and a big annual meeting where the volunteers are given a gift of appreciation and introduced to what's up and coming in recognition. Another critical part of the recognition network is the suppliers – our wellness center, cafeteria, event coordination department and purchasing agent. We worked very hard to develop agreements that were mutually beneficial and guaranteed long-term partnerships. Finally, we worked to establish a partnership with management, specifically those managers who would actively support and participate in the recognition process and provide the motivation and momentum to keep the processes focused. The entire network consists of approximately 150 people – 1.5% of the corporate population. These individuals are instrumental to sustaining the recognition effort.

9. *Address management's concern on 'abuse'.*

Part of management's concern prior to the pilot was that the systems would be abused. In their minds, *abuse = overuse*, friends collaborating for fun and profit. It turned out that in four years, only once did such collusion occur. It probably cost more to track the system than it did to cover the abuse! The tracking did reveal another type of abuse – lack of use. Our goal was to recognize 100% of the employee population. When lack of use was identified, we tried to give a personal presentation to the department in question, to somehow arrange to thank them or involve them in a recognition event, or to invite certain individuals in the organization to celebrations.

10. *Provide a clear tie to your corporation's quality initiatives.*

    We had a TQM initiative that called out recognition as the ninth step of a standardized quality improvement process. On introducing the recognition process, everyone was given a mug imprinted with this process on the side. Recognition was in bold print. Employees were encouraged to use the process to reduce costs, improve quality or reduce cycle time and to use the new recognition process to celebrate success. In addition, a matrix was provided showing behaviors and practices which supported the corporate mission, strategies and goals.

These 10 strategies and tactics provided us with the foundations for successful implementation and for making recognition a part of daily work activities. 'Slow, but sure' and 'dramatic, not drastic' were our mottoes. Within three years, the system was fully operational throughout the corporation.

This implementation strategy will help ensure that your system is truly employee-driven and designed for the recipient's needs. It also addresses the resistance to change issues encountered by any new philosophy or change in work processes. In addition, your measurements can be used to convince skeptics who follow the old school of management style which believes any accomplishment is 'just their job', and that the only effective form of recognition involves competition, contests, judging, a formal banquet and winners and losers.

Administrating the Process

You will definitely need at least one person who exclusively works on recognition administration. The tasks are many, but the job is personally rewarding.

Our administrator is responsible for marketing, 'adminis-trivia', consulting, purchasing, accounting, benchmarking, process maintenance, management reporting, and event facilitation. Quite a list! Some of the tasks are as follows:

Marketing.

- Identifying areas of low usage and encouraging participation.
- Regular presentations at all employee meetings.
- News articles on success stories for the company newspaper.

'Adminis-trivia'.

- Mailing invitations.
- Certificates.
- Response to requests by E-mail, phone, FAX and mail.
- Keeping catalogs of specialty items.
- Screening nomination forms for completeness and placing participants on an invitation list for recognition event.
- Scheduling team rallies, team events and celebrations.
- Keeping the recognition network informed.

Consulting.

- Helping in management decision-making regarding type of recognition.
- Chairing the cross-functional team responsible for recognition.

- Answering questions.
- Serving as resident expert on recognition.

Purchasing.

- Working with suppliers to get samples of new awards.
- Setting up purchase orders.
- Maintaining a supply of gift certificates.
- Taking care of 'special orders'.

Accounting.

- Maintaining the recognition budget.
- Charging appropriate accounts for funds used.
- Ensuring there is ample funding for celebrations, awards, and supplies.

Benchmarking.

- Responding to external requests for information on our system.
- Continuous external research for ideas to enhance our system.

Process Maintenance.

- Maintaining supply of thank you cards and tokens.
- Working with artists to produce tokens, logos, etc.
- Maintaining award inventory.
- Rolling out new improvements to the processes.
- Updating the procedure manual.

Management Reporting.

- Monthly management reporting on cost per employee, preferred tools, number of teams recognized, etc.
- Identifying areas which are not using the recognition tools and those with success stories.

Event Facilitation.

- Conducting team rallies.
- Working to set up time and place for Team Excellence celebrations.
- Helping decorate for team events and celebrations.
- Ensuring that awards and certificates are at the right place at the right time with the correct spelling.
- Invitations and RSVPs.
- Serving as MC at the Team Excellence celebrations.

This is just a partial list. As you can see, this position requires someone with tenacity, creativity, a great disposition and sense of humor, and the ability to communicate well, both in writing and orally, to management and non-management.

Appointing a special administrator for recognition sends a message to the work force that management is serious about recognition. It is not an extra job for someone to pick up, not if you are committed to changing the way you operate your business. And, it is not a job that just any person can assume.

Where should the administrator report? As mentioned previously, we started our pilot in the manufacturing organization. The manufacturing VP was the sponsor. So, our administrator reported to him. Even after the tools and processes were deployed throughout the corporation, it was decided to keep this arrangement. The reasons behind this decision included:

- You would never think of having the manufacturing organization in charge of recognition; this reinforced the philosophy that recognition was everyone's responsibility, not just a management job or a task for the human resource's function. Also, recognition was supported by a cross-functional team, so why should it matter who the administrator reported to?

- This allowed for thinking outside of our paradigm. The normal functional organizations responsible for recognition would never have this new perspective and the new ideas. This allowed for great changes.

Measuring and Monitoring Your Recognition System

Whenever a change is implemented, a multitude of measurements are collected to ensure the validity of the new approach and to convince the skeptics to join forces with the rest of the team. This system was no different. In fact, the softer side of leadership and work skills often comes under greater scrutiny and suspicion, requiring even more evidence of effectiveness. Management had several measurement requirements for the pilot effort of this system due to the facts that the entire work force would now be empowered to initiate recognition and that the goal of this system was to recognize 100% of the population versus less than 2% that were recognized by the former system. The proposal involved a great risk in their minds, both to the budget and management discretion and power. The measures mandated at start-up included:

- *Usage.*

  How much are we spending, on what, where, and with which tool?

- *Abuse.*

  Who is over-using the privilege?

- *Costs.*

  How much is this costing us per person?

Our mission clearly needed other system attributes collected. We had specific challenges to meet if the system was to be deemed 'effective' in our eyes, including:

- A steady increase in the percentage of the population recognized with a goal of 100%.
- The ability to determine which tools were meaningful and well-received.
- To ensure that the recognition included those who were important to the recipient, whether it be management, family, friends or co-workers.
- To see if all seven characteristics that we had established for an effective recognition system were being met by each of the tools.
- To verify the timeliness of each tool.
- To have evidence that the deployment of the methods had reached all departments and areas.

To have an effective measurement system, we took both the management requirements and the goals established from our mission, and determined the answers to the the following questions:

1. What information and data do we need to collect? What questions do we need answered?
2. What decisions will we make from this data and information?
3. What format should we use to present the data?
4. How often should the data be presented?
5. How will we monitor the process?
6. What 'signals' will we react to?
7. How will improvement opportunities be identified and prioritized?
8. How will we confirm that our customers (the recipients) are satisfied?

Sounds like quite a feat! Here is an example of what was developed for the Team Excellence process. *Management requirements* were met by tracking dollars spent, sorted by the functional organization. This data collection addressed the need to know cost, usage and possible abuse. The *recognition team's measurement requirements* were met with a 12 question survey that they developed after creating a list of critical success factors. The survey is given to a random sampling of participants after each celebration. All data is plotted on a control chart. In addition, we provide the summary of these statistics formatted into bar charts to management. A survey is the best tool to determine whether participants and customers are satisfied with the recognition tool being used. The next three pages will show you this survey.

Team Excellence Survey

Date of attendance ____________

1. Did you bring a guest to the celebration? (Check appropriate box).

   ☐ Yes ☐ No

2. Was your guest:

   ☐ A friend
   ☐ A family member
   ☐ A co-worker
   ☐ Your manager
   ☐ Other (please identify}

3. Having my personal guest at the celebration made the recognition event more meaningful for me. (Circle degree of agreement).

   Strongly disagree 1 2 3 4 5 6 7 Strongly agree

4. What is your opinion of the award selection?

   Unsatisfied 1 2 3 4 5 6 7 Satisfied

   Which of the following items would you like to see added to the award selection? (Check 3).

   ☐ Stadium blanker
   ☐ Stadium seats
   ☐ Golf umbrella
   ☐ Cross pen and pencil set
   ☐ Attache case
   ☐ Leather backpack
   ☐ Other (please list) ____________

Team Excellence Survey

5. How would you rate the atmosphere at the Team Excellence celebration?

Negative experience	1	2	3	4	5	6	7	Very positive and motivating

6. Did the team presentations add to the event?

Not interesting	1	2	3	4	5	6	7	Very inform-ative; it is good to know what other teams are doing

7. My perception of the games and activities at the Team Excellence celebration was:

They added no value	1	2	3	4	5	6	7	They added greatly to my enjoyment

8. What was your perception of the recognition given by the guest speaker at the end of the celebration?

Superficial; no value added	1	2	3	4	5	6	7	Very sincere and motivating

9. Rate the quality of your meal:

Poor	1	2	3	4	5	6	7	Excellent

Team Excellence Survey

10. Rate this type of team recognition:

Unsatis-factory	1	2	3	4	5	6	7	Meaningful; made me feel appreciated

11. What did you like *best* about the Team Excellence celebration?

____

____

____

____

____

12. What did you like *least* about the Team Excellence celebration?

____

____

____

____

____

Please add any suggestions for improvements or ideas you may have for future events:

____

____

____

____

____

As you can see, everyone's measurement requirements are met. More importantly, the needs of the recipient are tracked and monitored. The recognition team uses the control charts to determine areas of improvement and reacts to 'out of control' points the same way they do with their other work processes. This serves to reinforce that recognition is a key business process, to be treated in the same fashion as any other work process.

Chapter 4

Most Frequently Asked Questions

"Achieving return on equity does not, as a goal, mobilize the most noble forces of our souls."

Lawrence Miller

Questions and Concerns

We have given several presentations and overviews over the past five years. The following questions and concerns have been addressed in these sessions and may help clarify the system for you:

How much does it cost?

At the first company where we implemented this recognition system, $100 per employee was budgeted. Last year, the actual average cost per employee was $94. This figure includes thank you cards and tokens, celebrations and awards, certificates, lapel pins, miscellaneous supplies, etc.

Where are the funds budgeted? By the individual line managers?

Our system was budgeted at the vice-presidential level for several reasons including:

- To reduce management fear, resistance to change and cutbacks incorporated to achieve a favorable budget variance.

  Usage by individual manager or department is virtually invisible. This eliminates the risk of 'robbing Peter to pay Paul' in individual budgets. There is no risk of designated funds being used accidentally or intentionally for another or the wrong purpose.

- To demonstrate commitment to recognition.

  The money is in a recognition bucket. The amount has been committed and is used only for recognition. The recognition process administrator maintains and monitors the use. Both management and non-management perceive this as upper-level management commitment, thus ensuring that the tool will be used consistently and appropriately.

- To make the administration simpler.

Only a handful of budgets need to be monitored and maintained versus hundreds. There are six VPs using our system at one company. If all management below them each had a budget, there would be in excess of 200 budgets to monitor.

- To limit the reporting requirements.

  As mentioned above, when only a handful of budgets are affected, the set of management reporting requirements and expectations is kept to a minimum. This prevents the recognition administrator from becoming a 'slave to many masters'. Information is given at the staff meetings of the involved vice presidents to be disseminated through the management ranks.

I work in a white collar environment. What kind of recognition system and processes would I use?

This is a common mistake in judgment. In our initial development process, we reached a management impasse on this very issue. Our engineers, lawyers, accountants, sales people, marketing representatives, and management are just as human (well, most of the time!) as manufacturing assemblers, technicians and support associates. But, the thought was that the simplicity and value of the thank you card was unthinkable in these other environments, not to mention ball caps, silly celebrations, and tokens. I don't know who said 'people is people' or 'folks is folks', but that philosophy hits the nail on the head. Time proved that the other functional groups were equally as happy with these simple recognition techniques and that our concentration on the 'thought' and meaningful delivery far outweighed the value and type of award. This recognition system is not meant to compensate or replace a solid reward program. It is meant to show appreciation, approval and acknowledgment. Even though it is simple, it works!

What if someone uses the tool inappropriately?

There are several built-in controls, but if something slips through the cracks, the budget impact is minimal. We did have a case of someone writing a thank you and giving a token to a co-worker for setting up a blind date. We are still waiting to get positive metrics on that one! Even though setting up blind dates does not meet the criteria to make the business successful or job easier, this social concern obviously meant something to that employee and we know how our personal and professional lives are sometimes very difficult to separate. Three dollars in 'funny money', which was probably spent right at the company, was worth sacrificing our criteria in this instance. The important thing is to train your employee base, give examples of success stories and move on. Recognition is very personal and emotional and if this seemed to be the vehicle to address the need, so be it.

You have stated that the recognition should fit the recipient's needs. What if I receive the wrong award?

And what if your mother-in-law buys you a birthday or Christmas present you don't like? Do you say, "I didn't want this!" No. If your manners are intact, you accept the gift graciously and try to exchange it later or keep it, realizing that she was trying to be good to you. But, as we know, not everyone has the social grace we expect. Several individuals have asked to exchange awards and the recognition process administrator tries to accommodate these requests. When a team is involved, however, we ask that the entire group selects one recognition tool. The celebration would lose its impact if only half the team participated.

Have you seen any situations of flagrant abuse?

The most abused system is cash awards. Often, managers would use the cash awards to augment their employee's compensation, specifically when a large quantity of overtime was being worked and the employee was salaried.

The recognition tools in this book had one case of abuse on the token system over a four-year period and one questionable project recognized at the Team Excellence celebration. In the token system, there were two friends regularly exchanging several tokens per week.

This was stopped through management awareness and communication. We had established a very time consuming process of monitoring token usage when we initiated the system, for management expected blatant abuses. Over four years with six thousand employees using the system, only once did this occur. In fact, it probably cost more to track the system this closely than the abuse itself. Empowering people does require a certain amount of risk, but you will find that 99% of the people take responsibility seriously and will exceed your expectations if given the chance. The most valuable thing we learned from this tracking system was who was not using the system. When you are shooting for recognition of 100% of your employee base, lack of use is abuse. We were able to revisit these areas and try to get them excited about the system.

What obstacles did you have to overcome during implementation?

We faced several obstacles our first time out, but the two with the greatest impact included:

1. We had asked each functional organization to clearly define the qualities and practices that they considered recognizable. Most of these areas just used the examples provided as a guide. A greater benefit would have been realized had they taken the time to tell their organizations exactly what their specific organization wanted to accomplish and how. If you are involved in a TQM initiative, three things to focus on would be quality of your product/service, costs, and cycle time. It is greatly beneficial to have your specific goals communicated and an entire organization working to achieve them.

2. Several of the managers did not want to recognize their reports for anything that they were being paid for. The attitude was: "This is their job!" Well, yes. It is our job. But, one can complete a job with enthusiasm or with the minimum effort. One can offer new ideas for operating or just keep doing it the old way for the same

pay. In my mind, this is synonymous with customer satisfaction – do we simply address the expectation or do we try to delight the customer?

What is the ROI?

Guess what? We don't know! Return-on-investment is hard to quantify since the greatest benefits are in facilitating change more efficiently and effectively, improving morale and the quality of work life, and building self-esteem and company pride. Yet, all of these things can affect the success of your business. The quote at the beginning of this section says it all. Although we can't specifically quantify the difference in a dollar amount or return-on-investment ratio, we can say from personal experience that feeling good about our work enhances our product and service. At one Team Excellence celebration, the participating five teams saved over $4 million dollars. At the next celebration, approximately $300,000 was saved.

Would these teams have developed their process improvements without Team Excellence? Maybe. But the average cost of the celebration is only $1400. A drop in the bucket. And the celebrations are measured through a random sampling of participants for several criteria, one of which is: "Was this form of recognition meaningful to you?" On a scale of 1 to 7, with 7 being the highest rating, this question has an average score of 6.3+ for over three years. Most of the benefits to this type of recognition system are intangible, but consider a few to see if you think they are worth the investment:

- Sharing of information/improved communication.
- Better deployment of success stories and unique methods of problem-solving.
- Closure and encouragement to get started again.
- Reinforcement of desirable behaviors and practices.
- Happier, motivated and energetic work force.

- Inclusion of family, friends and those behind the scenes in the recognition process.
- Development of new relationships and a better professional network.
- Improved existing relationships with everyone involved in the work process.
- Management exposure.

And the list goes on and on . . .

Were there any benefits you didn't foresee?

Yes. People were not aware of some of the services our company provided through our recreation association, wellness center and business gifts. Business in these internal corporate functions literally went through the ceiling. Having these functions and their programs as a redemption option for tokens, for example, encouraged the employee population to take wellness classes, such as stress management, smoking cessation and diet planning. Improved service with support groups also resulted from the thanks process. In working with one support organization, I was often given a commit date 90 days in the future. The first time I received their service within two weeks, I delivered a thank you card and a gift certificate to the individual who had provided the service while she was eating lunch in the cafeteria with all her co-workers. As I was handing her my gift, I told her how much I appreciated the timeliness of her response. The next request I gave to this function was turned around within twenty-four hours. My requests received the same priority as the CEOs!

Hopefully, these questions and answers have helped to clarify the system and associated processes for you. A better tactic would be for you to just jump in and get your feet wet. Our challenge to you is to buy a box of thank you cards and write one at the end of each work day until the box is empty. Try writing one to a peer, a manager, a customer and a supplier, if possible. Write us a letter and let us know what you perceived the results to be. Did you feel good? Did it positively affect the recipient? Do you feel your relationship has improved? Write to:

Positive Strokes
5023 West 120th Avenue #128
Broomfield, Colorado 80020

Chapter 5

Conclusion

"You have to have your heart in the business, and the business in your heart."

Thomas J. Watson, Sr.

"In recognizing the humanity of our fellow human beings, we pay ourselves the highest tribute."

Thurgood Marshall

"Lack of something to feel important about is almost the greatest tragedy a man can have."

Arthur E. Morgan

Closing

There has been much speculation about the decline of American business during the second half of the twentieth century. All kinds of theories, quality philosophies and practices, and consultants rose from this upheaval. Most of these programs and processes were good, from SPC to JIT. But, tools are only as good as the individual or group applying them. We lost in the marketplace when we stopped caring – caring about the quality of our products and services, caring about our employees, caring about our co-workers, and caring about our customers and suppliers. We took for granted that these relationships would not require our constant attention. We became superficial and automatic in our dealings and communications. We concentrated on the almighty buck. *We were wrong!*

Pride in workmanship cannot be measured on a control chart. Creativity and innovation are not identifiable in a design of experiments. Honesty, sincerity and manners cannot be delivered 'just-in-time'. Yet all of these personal qualities are necessary to operate competitively and successfully.

Let's consider the potential gains of 'caring':

Caring about the quality of our work.

- Improved sales.
- Improved revenues.
- Improved stock price.
- Improved marketplace position.

Caring about our employees.

- Lower attrition rate.
- Less stress-related illnesses.
- Fewer attendance problems.
- Increased company pride; employees that go to other companies to share their success stories, not to turn in a résumé.

- Improved morale and quality of work life.
- More effort from employees to go the 'extra mile'.

Caring about co-workers.

- Improved teamwork.
- Improved communication.
- Elimination of functional barriers.
- Elimination of barriers to peak performance.
- Improved work environment.
- Less sabotage and competition between peers.

Caring about customers.

- Drives repeat business.
- Improved satisfaction levels.
- Can be deciding factor for selecting supplier, if prices and services are comparable.
- Can determine survival.

Caring about suppliers.

- Long-term partnerships.
- Improved performance.
- Can gain priority service.
- Reduction in supplier base.

And, what about the other side of the coin? What are the disadvantages to 'caring'?

Zero

There are none.

We have all kinds of quality improvement processes and problem-solving tools which can dramatically decrease costs, reduce cycle time and improve the quality of our products and services. But, a dramatic culture change is required to gain the greatest benefit from these initiatives. Approaching our work systematically and improving our services and products continuously is a major change in our *modus operandi.* Like any other change, it will require a well-thought strategy and planning. There are two critical considerations or change agents required to drive such a transformation – recognition and communication. All kinds of complicated ways can be developed to fulfill this requirement. Using the KISS formula (Keep It Simple, Stupid!), it is evident that a 'thank you' card offers both communication and recognition.

The process for developing your recognition system is equally as simple:

1. Determine what you want to achieve – your vision, mission, strategy, goals and objectives. Communicate to everyone.

2. Determine what behaviors and practices support the things you want to achieve. Communicate to everyone.

3. Select your tools; check against the seven recognition criteria. Communicate to everyone.

4. Show you care – recognize *whenever* the behaviors and practices are exhibited. Develop tools that are easy, available, that can be initiated by anyone and address every possible situation which supports what you want to achieve. Strive to recognize 100%.

5. Measure, monitor and continuously improve your recognition processes. Communicate to everyone.

Recently, experts have begun questioning the value of quotas, incentives, MBOs, pay for performance and all of the different reward systems we have implemented in our pursuit of a motivated work force. We believe, however, there is not a dollar amount in existence that can replace the social and psychological need of human beings to feel appreciated. Most of us go to work to satisfy a financial need, so it is a fact that a sound compensation system is a necessity. But, what is the difference between an employee who is happy with their work environment and the one who dreads walking through the door every morning? The difference is the same as that between mediocrity and excellence, 'just enough' and 'beyond expectation', rote performance of job tasks and creative, outstanding contribution, the least and the most, displaying a work skill and demonstrating unknown talents. In *My Friend Pavarotti*, as quoted by Candido Bonvicini, Luciano Pavrotti states:

> *"You never know what little bundle of encouragements artists carry around with them, what little pats on the back from what hands, what newspaper clipping, what word of hope from what teacher. I suppose that the so-called faith in ourselves is the foundation of our talent, but I am sure these encouragements are the mortar that holds it together."*

The choice is yours. Each one of us can make a difference in our work environment, with or without a formal recognition system. It is as simple as saying 'thank you' and genuinely meaning it.

Acknowledgments

"Never doubt that a small group of thoughtful, committed people can change the world; indeed it is the only thing that ever has."

Margaret Mead

Thank You

Since this book is all about appreciation and saying 'thank you', it is only appropriate that we thank those special people who have touched our lives and left a lasting impression of goodness and a vision of what we could become. All of these people believed in us and gave us the constant support and guidance we needed to make our efforts successful, our philosophy known and our hard work beneficial. They are our lifelong partners, providing us with unconditional love and friendship, and we love you all. Our hope is that we will be given the opportunity to return your 'gifts' in this short lifetime. Until then, all of you hold a very special place in our hearts and minds.

Thank you, Jim Glasscock (husband and friend)

Even the motivators needed motivating. You served as an inspiration to both of us. When we would slow down, you would confront us with the importance of what we were trying to accomplish. When there was something to be done that you could help with, we didn't even have to ask, you anticipated the need and did it. Your importance to us goes way beyond this book. You are a living example of a good husband and true friend.

Thank you, Jack and Peggy Gram and Leon and Helen Shafer (our parents)

We heard a speaker once at a forum state: "Ninety-six percent of the American population is from dysfunctional families. The other 4% are in denial!" This just isn't true. We both come from loving homes which provided us with the foundation blocks to build our philosophy and live our lives – honesty, sincerity, warmth, charity and unconditional love. Without these qualities, we would be nothing and have nothing. Hopefully, we can share these gifts with those who have been deprived. Your investment has already yielded a great return. Your caring and sharing will be reflected in this book and all of our work to come. We know God holds a special place in heaven for all of you.

Thank you, Dustin, Jessica, Todd, Beau and Kelly (our children)

You sacrificed your time with us without complaint. You understood when fast food was dinner and vacations were spent working. We have been blessed with children who steadfastly maintained the lines of communication, sending cards to us on the road and making sure they were home when we called. We hope you are as proud of us as we are of you. Without your sacrifices, we could not have made our dream come true.

Thank you to our special friends

Dick Ralston, vice-president of manufacturing at StorageTek

You believed in us and took us under your wing. You not only piloted our processes, but actively worked and participated to ensure their success. We know that sometimes you had your doubts about our direction and methods, but you trusted our instincts and empowered us to move forward. You are the manager everyone dreams of having.

Kathy Ralston, our editor and friend

Your editing skills added to our message. You are not only a gracious and beautiful woman, but one full of spirit and resourcefulness. We are better people for having known you.

Dan Murray, work associate and president of our fan club

There are not too many people we chance to work with that sincerely celebrate the success of others and willingly enhance their efforts to succeed. You gave us encouragement, ideas and support. You are much more than a peer, a friend or a co-worker. You exemplify principle-driven and value-based leadership. We hope we can emulate your fine qualities in everything we do.

Gerry Benner and Nancy Benner, true visionaries

You both were always available to help with computer graphics, editing, brainstorming for activities, or just to give us the old, "You're on the right track" speech. It isn't very often such talent and insight comes in a pair. We were lucky to have your help and honored just to know you.

Jeff Ketelhut, AMGEN Corporation

You came. You saw. You adopted. Your benchmarking team from AMGEN opened our eyes to the potential of expanding our vision beyond our own four walls. You continuously provided us with moral support, from 1200 miles away. Quite a feat! We are glad chance and circumstances allowed our paths to cross.

StorageTek Recognition Network

Several individuals and subteams worked to develop tools shown in this book. Without this network of supporters and volunteers, the dream would not have become a reality. It is seldom that a grass-roots approach ever reaches the magnitude of this effort. You were the *right* people for the *right* job. You knew that 'right gives you might' and that sometimes in real life, like in the old movies, the good guys win.

Thank you, God

Without You, none of this would be possible. Without our faith, our lives and work would not have meaning.